Just Hand Over
the **CHOCOLATE**
and *No One*
Will Get Hurt

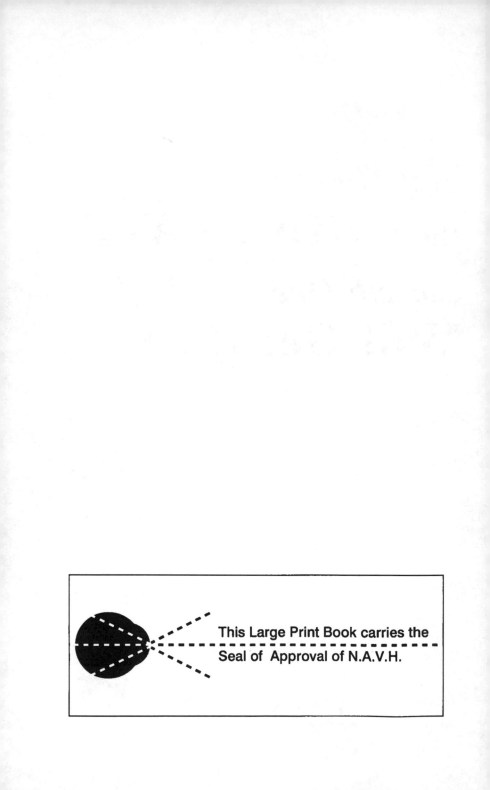

This Large Print Book carries the
Seal of Approval of N.A.V.H.

Just Hand Over the **CHOCOLATE** and *No One* Will Get Hurt

KAREN SCALF LINAMEN

Walker Large Print • Waterville, Maine

Published in 2002 by arrangement with Baker Book House.

The text of this Large Print edition is unabridged.
Other aspects of the book may vary from the original edition.

Set in 16 pt. Plantin by Warren S. Doersam.

Printed in the United States on permanent paper.

ISBN 1-4104-0022-0 (lg. print : sc : alk. paper)

To Linda Holland,
who not only helps shepherd my career,
but also holds my hand in matters of
life, laughter, and mental health.
Best yet, she's one of my few friends who
will admit that she knows, as I do,
what eating an entire box of Cap'n
Crunch cereal will do to the roof of
your mouth,
which is just one of the many reasons I
love her.

Contents

Acknowledgments

I owe a debt of gratitude to the usual suspects at Revell, including Dwight Baker, Twila Bennett, Dan Baker, Linda Holland, and the editorial staff. This is my third book with Revell, and I am not only grateful for the confidence they place in my work, but also for the friendships that have developed over the past four years.

I would also like to acknowledge the very dear friends who make up the Friday Morning Breakfast Club. These women have seen me at my best and my worst — and they're still willing to return my calls. Go figure. I thank God for Cherie Spurlock, Nancy Rottmeyer, Darla Talley, and Linda Douglas.

Other big-time encouragers include friend and confidante Beth Forester, master encourager Mike Talley, my talented husband, Larry, and two incredible friends who also happen to be my parents,

Gene and Geri Scalf. I am also blessed to acknowledge my sister Michelle Willett who loves me no matter what trouble I get into, and my sister Renee Berge with whom I share more fond memories of chocolate binges than either of us would be willing to divulge.

These are, indeed, just a few of the folks who have held my hand, held me accountable, and helped me hold my chin up when my own life has felt too busy, bruised, or blue. And of course, in the process, they have not only enriched my life, but given me lots of great material for this book as well. I am in their debt.

Introduction

Whenever I tell folks that I've written a book about coping with stress, crisis, depression, or PMS, I get immediate interest. After all, what woman has not lived through these experiences and what husband does not have the scars to prove it?

But when I share the title of this book, one of two things happens.

If I'm talking to a man and I happen to mention that my newest book is called *Just Hand Over the Chocolate and No One Will Get Hurt,* he smiles politely. But I can see that he is still waiting for the punch line.

If I am speaking to a woman, however, her eyes begin to glow and her face reflects a conflicting blend of agony and delight and finally, yes, even gratitude. Her death grip on my arm speaks silent volumes. Her message is clear: "Yes! Finally! Someone who understands!"

When it comes to chocolate and stress,

women don't need a punch line.

We get the connection.

The fact is, when we are feeling anxious or blue, chocolate seems to call our names, doesn't it? One explanation might be found in the fact that chocolate stimulates production of something called phenylethylamine. Nicknamed the "love molecule," phenylethylamine is the hormone that creates that intoxicating "in love" feeling that sweeps us off our feet when romance is new.

Is it any wonder we're crazy about our chocolate?

Chocolate may be the next best thing to sex, but it can't do miracles. The fact is, there are times when life feels overwhelming and not even a jumbo bag of M&M's will do the trick.

Of course, sometimes you and I feel overwhelmed for no greater reason than the fact that we're not getting enough sleep or it's THAT time of the month. On the other hand, you and I can feel overwhelmed because of very significant reasons such as over-overcommitment, depression, poor boundaries, crisis, or past or present hurts.

Whether your problem is fleeting or deep-seated, in the pages of this book you will find fifteen actions that can help you feel better physically, emotionally, and/or spiritually. Now, I'll be the first to admit that some of these ideas are quick fixes. Singing TV-land theme songs, for example, cannot save a marriage or help you forgive a past hurt. Other chapters, however, provide long-range solutions to help salve even the deepest wounds.

In the pages of this book, you will learn, among other things:

- Where to find the words to all eight stanzas of the *Gilligan's Island* theme song

- How to get the most out of a fine whine

- How to rekindle and pursue your dreams

- What Prozac and potting soil have in common

- Nine signs that you desperately need a vacation

- Five things you can say to a friend when you're hurting and you need some encouragement

- Seven ways to clean up your life and put new bounce in your step

- How to enjoy rejuvenating private moments no matter how busy your schedule

- Three lies that can keep you chained to a nasty grudge

- What Elvis and E.T. have to do with clinical depression

- Three no-fail tips that will leave you feeling young again

- How healthy boundaries are like good neighbors

If you've ever felt like your sanity was in a body bag, if you think Rolaids is a major food group, if the nervous tic in your eye prompts strange men to wink back and ask for your phone number, take heart! You hold in your hands your very own collection of joy-boosters, stress-busters, hope-builders, warm fuzzies, quick fixes, good ideas, and long-term solutions. Pick and choose your way through them. And may God bless and encourage you as you begin taking steps that will allow you to experience greater joy and wholeness in your life!

1

Mary, Mary, Quite Contrary . . . How Does Your Garden Grow?

Plants at my house don't have a chance.

One day my eleven-year-old daughter announced to one of my friends, "Mom likes fake plants because they're the only ones she can't kill."

"That's not true, Kaitlyn," I objected. "You'd be surprised how many fake plants have died in my care."

The most common cause of death for fake plants at my house is asphyxiation by dust. This is because the thought of dusting 687 individual silk ficus tree leaves ranks right up there with paying taxes or going in for my annual gynecological checkup.

Of course, real plants die interesting deaths at my house too. I once had a ficus tree in my bedroom that suffered a particularly gruesome and prolonged demise. I finally decided to put it out of its misery on a day my parents were due to fly in for a visit. My mom is great with plants — she can grow anything. Not wanting her to learn of my epic horticultural failure, I asked my husband to stash the dead tree in the garage before we drove to the airport to meet my parents' plane.

Several hours later — confident my bedroom was void of incriminating evidence — I invited my folks into the room to see a new piece of furniture. We were several feet into the room when I stopped in my tracks. In the corner, where the tree had once stood, was a circle of dead leaves. It spoke as eloquently as any chalk outline at a crime scene. I halfway expected Columbo to emerge from the closet, fingerprinting kit in hand. A quick dusting of the watering can would convict me for sure: The glaring absence of my fingerprints would give any D.A. more than enough evidence for a quick verdict.

The plant that has lived the longest in my home is a potted plant my husband bought for me nearly three years ago when I was in the hospital giving birth to our youngest child. In other words, this leafy wonder is nothing less than a horti-miracle. It has, indeed, exceeded the expected life span of any plant that has ever had the misfortune of being under my care. Some of the leaves still even look nice. And I think the roots coming through the bottom of the pot and melding into the tabletop add a unique touch. I suspect the ensemble will bring big bucks if I ever decide to sell it at a garage sale.

I think the primary problem here is that plants require water, which is just not something I think about on a daily basis. I tend to water my plants during leap years or on evenings my husband lets me hold the TV remote, whichever comes first.

Which leads me to the subject of evolution. You know what I'm talking about: I'm talking about that ridiculous theory that claims that living things, in the face of a hostile environment, can adapt and evolve and survive against the odds. This is a lie. Oh sure, it might explain the tenacious existence of cockroaches and dinner-hour phone salesmen, but in general, organisms that we try to exterminate do not evolve their way to better living. If that kind of evolution were possible, plants in my home would have learned how to speak by now. Then they could pester me for water the way my kids pester me for things *they* need to survive (like Beanie Babies and compact discs).

No, my plants just sit there, silent, and watch me not water them. So you see, I can't be held entirely to blame for their demise. They never even lift a leaf to help.

But there is an encouraging sign in all of this. The good news is that I even have plants in my home. There were several years in my life when that would have been virtually impossible.

Prozac and Potting Soil

There were a number of years when I lived my life numb and overwhelmed. In the grip of then-undiagnosed clinical depression, it was all I could do to get through my days taking care of the most basic needs of my family. Kaitlyn was a preschooler at the time, and as long as I managed to shepherd her through her day emotionally and physically intact, I considered myself successful. There seemed little room in my life for "luxuries" like friendships or cooking meals or getting out of bed when I didn't have to, much less the acquisition of houseplants or garden blooms that would levy even more demands on my already overwhelmed system.

Who knows? Maybe I did the right thing, stripping my world of everything save the one nonnegotiable responsibility of caring for my daughter. I functioned in this emotional cocoon until crisis brought my marriage and my emotional health to a serious crossroad. Luckily for me, the trail-thin footpath we took at that point led ultimately to healing and wholeness.

I wonder, though, what seeds of healing might have been sown had I mustered the energy to plant something.

Something beautiful, like wildflowers.

Something fruitful, like kitchen herbs.

Something ambitious, like morning glories.

Something forgiving, like a cactus!

You see, I know something now that I didn't know then. Back then, I was afraid that fragile growing things would be "takers" rather than "givers." I thought they would demand things of me I couldn't afford, like time and energy. I thought they would prove to be a liability rather than an asset in my sad, bruised world. I never even gave them a chance.

Potting Soil Therapy

Now I know that the relationship we share with our photosynthesizing friends is not a one-sided affair. They need us to take care of them, it's true. But sometimes in the process, they can nurture us as well. When we are stressed by daily living, over-whelmed by the arrows and wounds that come our way, or perplexed by a slippery problem for which there seems no good answer, the act of caring for our rooty buddies can help us tap into relief, restoration, and even creativity.

There are lots of reasons why gardens and houseplants can make a positive difference in our lives. And I'm not even suggesting that you and I turn into the next Martha Stewart or Neil Sperry. Even a casual interest in a few no-fail plants can reap rewards. What kinds of benefits are ours when we plant something? Let's look at a few:

Wake-up Call to the Senses

Let's face it. There's something about

plunging your hands into a mess of potting soil that sort of wakes up the senses, doesn't it? Now grant it, one of the senses that it awakens for some people is a feeling of "Ugh, gross." But bear with me for a moment.

Even if you don't have a green thumb, planting something provides a rich array of sensory experiences. There's the pungent fragrance of wet earth, the cool massage as you work your hands into the loamy soil, the gritty song of a clay pot when it shifts in its saucer, and the bright colors and fragile beauty of the transplanted bloom. When we exercise our senses, we feel more alive. Indeed, a handful of pleasant sensory delights is like a gentle massage of the soul.

Sense of Accomplishment and Progress

Do you ever feel like a hamster on a treadmill? Sometimes it seems as though, try as I might, I just can't make any progress. The dishes I washed yesterday are dirty again today. I managed to meet a critical deadline last week, but today there's a new fire to be extinguished. The ten pounds I worked so hard to lose must have my beeper number, because they managed to find me again in no time at all.

Sometimes when I'm feeling blue, one thing that will perk me right up is the glow that comes with accomplishment. The satisfaction that comes with progress. Do you want virtually immediate accomplishment? Visible results in ten minutes or less? Then weed a small flower bed (be sure to water it first and the weeds pull out easily). Or transplant a flower. Or snip some backyard blooms for your kitchen table. Quick tasks, every one — and yet doing them, you'll enjoy a sense of accomplishment.

A Connection with Nature

I planted cherry tomatoes this year. This was actually my first foray into vegetable gardening since childhood. One day, when my plants were about knee-high, I noticed a black and green visitor clamped to a stem. Then I noticed a whole community of them. Caterpillars.

Plucking them willy-nilly from the stems, I ended up with about a dozen pests wriggling in the bottom of a butter tub. Now here's the amazing thing. Guess what I was feeling, emotionally, as I watched the little buggers climbing blindly all over each other.

Disgust?

Try again.

Delight!

I know, it surprises me, too, but there it was. Delight!

After all, when had I last studied the tentative dance of one of God's metamorphosing critters? Not since grade school, I can assure you. And I had forgotten just how fascinating they really are!

I called to my daughters and we spent the next hour playing with our new friends. We progressed from daring each other to touch them, to letting them walk on our hands, to designing caterpillar mazes on Kacie's play table.

In the end, we let them all go free. After all, they had served us well, ushering us into a place of wonder and delight.

A Creative Outlet

Yes, our gardens can make us feel more connected with nature. But they can also provide a creative outlet as we paint a flower bed with textures, shapes, and hues.

As a mom, I also try to incorporate creative, whimsical touches to delight my kids. When two-year-old Kacie, for example, fell in love with a concrete lion statue in my mom's garden, I searched three nurseries until I found a similar cat to prowl beneath a fruit tree in my yard. There is a giant resin toad next to my hydrangeas, and a sundial among the daylilies. I found a bird feeder in the shape of a smiling sun with two hands cupped beneath his chin, and I hung him on a brick wall within view of both the garden and the den window.

Harriet Crosby, in her book *A Place Called Home* (Thomas Nelson, 1997), has written, "A garden soothes troubled hearts, delights the senses, feeds the body, and offers us a second Eden in which to play and rest."

Get creative. Have fun. Play a little. You'll be amazed how great it feels.

Lessons about Time and Seasons

There's something healing about the rhythm of nature. In particular, I find a lot of comfort in the ebb and flow of the seasons.

Now, I didn't always know about seasons. Born and raised in southern California, I used to think that West Coast living had the best weather. Then Larry and I married and spent two years in the Midwest, and I discovered this phenomenon called seasons.

When we moved back to California, I realized something was missing. Our first Christmas back home, I hung our outdoor Christmas lights wearing a T-shirt and shorts. The same Saturday I went Christmas shopping, my husband mowed the lawn.

It's not just that California doesn't have a winter; it doesn't have a fall, either, because the weather doesn't get cold enough to change the colors of the leaves.

I'll admit, one autumn I spotted some richly colored leaves. I was in a craft shop and they were selling these plastic bags of fake fall leaves. I bought six bags and sprinkled them on our lawn.

Larry didn't think it was too funny.

The point is, there is something satisfying, rejuvenating, comforting about the seasons of the year. Seasons remind me that there is a time and a season for everything, and that "this too shall pass." They remind me that there is a pulse, a sequence, a journey set into motion by the hand of God himself. The seasons remind me daily of God's timing, of nature, of the ebb and flow of life.

When I'm stressed or going through a tough time, puttering around in the backyard puts me in touch with those seasons like little else can. Preparing the soil . . . planting seeds . . . providing nutrients for growth . . . trimming dead leaves . . . battling weeds . . . enjoying beauty . . . watching something that was beautiful become dormant or even die . . . observing new life and new growth once springtime has come . . .

Preparation. Nurture. Beauty. Struggle. Dormancy and even death. New growth, new hope, and new life.

It's powerful. You know why? Because the cycle is one that is repeated in my own life over and over again.

After all, plants and trees start small, just like we do. They have seasons of fruitfulness. They also have dormant times when they don't seem to be doing anything worthwhile . . . except recovering, resting, and waiting for a new season of growth.

Just like you and me.

And have you ever thought about the place where a seed begins to germinate? It's a dark place, away from light and fresh

26

air, void of colors and empty of happy sounds. I've been in places like that, haven't you? Dark places of the soul where we feel isolated from all things bright and beautiful. And yet, out of the darkness comes new life, new beginnings, new wisdom.

Getting in touch with nature is healing because, indeed, in some fashion it reveals to us the potential of our own tomorrows. After all, if a hydrangea plant that seems so lifeless and dry can blossom into such exquisite life and color . . . if a troubled winter sky, the color of bruises and weeping great drops of rain, can find cause to adorn herself with spring sunshine, fresh scents, and breathtaking rainbows . . . if the earthbound caterpillar can find a way to soar on butterfly wings, a new creature in every fashion . . . then guess what? There's hope for you and me. Whatever our trials, whatever our struggles, tomorrow holds the chance for new growth. A fresh start. A reason to celebrate the wonders of life.

There Is a Master Plan

Finally, what else do I learn from my garden?

How 'bout the fact that there's a Master Gardener, someone who orchestrates the seasons, commands the sun, coaxes the rain. Someone who knows how to pack eighty feet of morning glory vine into a seed smaller than a nail clipping. Someone who enlists the help of birds and bees, ladybugs and caterpillars, spiders and earthworms to tend to the green things he has set into motion.

Best of all, someone who says, "Look at the field lilies and how well they're dressed! Hey, if I take such good care of the flowers that are here today and gone tomorrow, don't you think I can take care of you?"

Do green, living things shudder at the mention of your name? Have you been known to kill even the sturdiest of silk plants? Based on your personal experience, would you categorize *Better Homes and Gardens* as a work of fiction? Have your most successful gardening efforts to date been confined to growing Chia pets and cultivating mold in your refrigerator?

Take heart. You, too, can experience the joy of gardening.

Call a local nursery. Ask for the names of some no-fail plants that thrive in your climate zone. Here's some advice I gleaned from a nursery near me:

E-Z Grow Garden Staples
impatiens (shade)
caladiums (shade)
light leaf begonias (shade)
dark leaf begonias (shade or
    sun)

moss rose (sun)
purslane (sun)
periwinkle (sun)
lantana (sun)
Mexican heather (sun)
pansies (sun)

Neglect-Proof Houseplants
pothos
sansevieria
philodendron
dracaena
dieffenbachia

2

Minivacations Even a Travel Agent Could Love

How do you know whether or not you need a vacation? In case you aren't quite sure, I've compiled a list designed to help you determine whether you should (a) arrange some time to get away from it all, or (b) go on running yourself into the ground.

If you find yourself exhibiting any number of the following symptoms, then this chapter is definitely for you.

So here they are, nine signs that you need a vacation:

If you find yourself looking forward to your next dentist appointment as a chance to sit and relax for a half hour . . .

If your need for Rolaids is exceeded only by your craving for chocolate . . .

If the nervous tic in your eye prompts strange men to wink back and ask you for your phone number . . .

> then you might be in need of a vacation.

If the music you listened to on your last getaway was Barry Manilow — on eight-track . . .

If you'd love for Calgon to take you away, but the piles of laundry in the hallway keep blocking you from getting into your bathroom . . .

If your husband is beginning to fear that the P in PMS just might stand for *permanent* . . .

> then there's a good chance that you're in need of a vacation.

If the last time you got away for dinner and a movie, you thought John Travolta looked pretty good in those white pants . . .

If the closest you've come to a vacation in the past six months has been cruising the information highway . . .

If your days are so full you can't even find time to wash your hair *and* shave your legs during the same shower . . .

then there's no question. You definitely need a vacation.

Ever Need a Vacation to Recover from a Vacation?

Sometimes my husband will surprise me with the following suggestion: "Let's get away this weekend. Maybe get a hotel or something."

He thinks that these two phrases will immediately usher me into a euphoric state. The state, however, that I am most likely to visit upon hearing these phrases is the Great State of Panic. This is because the words running through my mind at that moment are not "Jacuzzi" or "room service" or even "sex," but "baby-sitter" and "no clean clothes" and "What about the chicken I just defrosted?"

Why is it that the process of getting out the door to "get away and relax" usually provides a level of logistical challenge that even U.S. military intelligence would find daunting? The fact that the Army routinely transports hundreds of thousands of soldiers and tons of military hardware from one end of the world to the other is not nearly the logistical accomplishment of, say, taking three kids, a spouse, and a dog on a cross-country trip to Disneyworld.

No, getting away from it all is not, by nature, a stress-free endeavor. Too often, I need a vacation to recover from my vacation.

Sometimes my husband suggests that we go camping. Now, despite fond memories of family camping experiences from my childhood, I am not usually overjoyed to hear this suggestion from my spouse. This is because my idea of the ideal vacation is not spending three days doing exactly what I do at home — meaning cooking and cleaning up — but without the benefit of things like hot water, refrigerators, and the microwave.

Once, we went camping and planned a menu of creative meals designed to be cooked over an open fire. When we got to our campsite, we discovered a "fire ban" due to dry weather conditions. We spent every meal at a Kentucky Fried Chicken two miles into town. It didn't do much to make us feel like we had "gotten away" from civilization, but it did get me out of trying to scrub grease off tin plates with cold water.

The very first time Larry took me camping, we had been married about six months. We arrived at our campsite after dark only to discover that we had forgotten to pack any sleeping bags. Now, even newlyweds who view life through a romantic haze will become grumpy if asked to sleep in a tent pitched on root-riddled ground, with only sweaters and newspaper to keep them warm.

We took another camping trip when I was six months pregnant. Now this might not seem like a big deal to any man who is reading this, but any woman who has experienced pregnancy will realize immediately the problem to which I am referring. The good news is that by the end of that first night I was so accustomed to the trail I hardly needed the flashlight to make the quarter-mile hike to the bathroom.

Finding Time for Memorable Getaways

Now, despite the cynic in me, I don't really believe that *bona fide* vacations should be eliminated from our busy lives. Yes, they are a lot of work and, yes, sometimes they provide fertile ground for chaos and disaster. The good news is that comedy is often merely tragedy plus time. See? Sixteen years later I'm laughing about the missing sleeping bags. Believe it or not, that incident has become a warm family memory. Okay, maybe warm is the wrong word, because I froze for three nights and gave my husband the cold shoulder for a week beyond that, but you know what I mean. It's a *fond* memory.

So maybe vacations are worth the effort after all. They provide adventure and togetherness and new perspectives. And even if our bodies come home jet-lagged or tired from hours in the car, very often our spirits come home renewed and refreshed. Vacations give us a chance to leave the beeper and fax machine at home and experience a too-brief respite from the responsibilities and pressures of our jobs. Not to mention photo opportunities you just don't get at home.

And the memories . . .

I still remember the vacation my extended family took to Corbin, Kentucky, where my dad spent a lot of his growing-up years. We visited relatives and cemeteries and even the swimming hole my dad frequented, "nekkid," as a kid. One day we set out to find Scalf, a tiny foothill village named after my relatives. There were three people in the front seat — my dad, mom, and daughter Kaitlyn, then four years old. There were three-and-a-half of us in the backseat — my sister Michelle, my pregnant sister Renee, and me. It was a little crowded, but we were in good spirits as we jolted over rutted dirt roads in search of treasure.

Before long we passed a wooden shack with a rusted washing machine in the front yard. A woman stood sweeping the crooked porch, and my dad slowed the car and rolled down the window. "Mornin'," he said, and I loved the way that, even after living forty-five years on the West Coast, he was unable to spend twenty-four hours in the South before relaxing into the musical drawl of his youth. "How far is it to a place called Scalf?"

The woman stopped sweeping. "This is it."

Around the next bend, we discovered a combination gas station, grocery store, and post office. The proprietor was a grizzled fella' who'd just as soon spit than smile. Between customers, he watched the weather change from the front porch of the little store, sitting on an upholstered bench that had been salvaged from the front seat of a Buick.

What wonderful memories I have of that trip. Even now I can close my eyes and remember the warmth of the Southern summer sun . . . the song of the crickets in the tall roadside grass . . . the images and sounds and smells.

Ah, yes. The smells.

During the ride home my sisters and I noticed a faint odor. Pungent. Unrecognizably familiar. Growing stronger with each passing mile. We looked at one another, raised our eyebrows, and shrugged our shoulders. Maybe we were nearing a factory. Surely the smell would diminish as we traveled!

Twenty minutes later, the odor was still there. I finally addressed my folks in the front seat.

"Are we going crazy back here, or is there a weird smell in here?"

My mom turned around. "I smell something, too. What is that?"

A brief search in the car failed to turn up a source.

Renee looked thoughtful. "It smells . . . almost like . . ."

Michelle wrinkled her nose. "Feet!"

All eyes suddenly were drawn to Kaitlyn. She was sitting between my parents in the front seat, relaxed and comfortable after our morning trek across the dusty Kentucky hillside. In fact, she had pulled her shoes off, propped her sweaty feet on the dashboard, and was cooling her toes in front of the air conditioner!

Another memory from the archives: the lively music of our laughter!

Yes, vacations have a lot to offer, after all.

Got a Minute? Take a Vacation!

Wouldn't it be nice if we could pack our bags whenever we needed a break from the routine stress of living? Unfortunately, finding time to get away for a week or even a weekend can prove daunting. When soccer games, piano recitals, doctor appointments, job demands, and school schedules mesh together in a tangled way, sometimes it's difficult to find a time when your family can leave town together, on the same day, at the same time.

I remember the day my husband called me from work and said, "I'm calling to reserve the second week in October, 1999, for a family vacation. I thought we could spend a week at a cabin in New Mexico."

Something about his request struck me as odd. Just to make sure, I looked at my calendar.

"1999," I said. "That's two years from now."

He said, "I know. I wanted to make sure everyone could make it."

If, like me, you've had to wait two years for your next family vacation, then you'll appreciate my idea. What if there were things we could do — small things that don't require huge commitments of time and money — that could give us small doses of the things we love best about vacations? What if we got in the habit of taking minivacations, if you will? What if a few minutes or hours — stolen from our daily routines — could leave us refreshed and revitalized in some fashion?

Have I been sampling the kitchen sherry? Hardly. Indeed, sometimes even a small break can pay big dividends. In fact, here are five ideas for minivacations even a travel agent could love.

Backyard Paradise

Not long ago I was feeling tired from the pressures of daily living. Not quite willing to go into my office and face the piles of paperwork that awaited me, I headed to my backyard to water a few plants.

And guess what I found?

Parched plants, sure. But what else?

Nature!

Bright magenta blooms on the morning glories . . . the chatter of bluebirds and martins and sparrows . . . the lazy waltz of white clouds across an azure sky . . . and the sound of my name being called by the hammock that swings between two cedar trees next to my back porch.

Moments later, floating beneath an evergreen canopy, all my problems faded into a simple awareness of the kiss of the sun on my legs, the caress of a breeze, the song of the wind chime on the porch.

Okay, I admit it. I fell asleep. Or maybe

half asleep. Because even in slumber, I was lazily aware of the magic of the warm September morning. Heading back into my office forty-five minutes later, I felt refreshed and relaxed.

My guess is that you've got a spot around your home that could double as a backyard paradise, too. What could you do to create a "getaway" feeling in your own backyard?

A **hammock** is a must-have. If you don't have cooperative tree trunks, purchase a hammock with its own stand.

Wind chimes. Don't settle for something from the dollar store with a tinny voice. I looked for months until I found just the right chime, with a haunting song that makes me think of dappled forest sunshine and the flirtatious laughter of a hidden brook. This particular chime cost thirty dollars — more than many others I'd looked at — but I'm glad I paid the price whenever I hear it dancing with the wind.

Textiles for comfort. Buy chair cushions and colorful throw pillows to soften wicker love seats, plastic chairs, or wooden furniture. Keep a cotton throw on hand in case breezes get too cool. A bright tablecloth draped at an angle over a picnic bench or patio table can create a festive sight. For easy access, I stash outdoor cushions and linens in a box near my back door, and just take some items with me when I go outside. It's amazing how inviting outdoor furniture can become with the help of some bright fabric!

Try some **coconut sun lotion** — with or without the sun! Want to feel far away from it all? Apply a little lotion before going outside — even if you're planning on sitting in the shade! The combination of certain fragrances and fond memories, after all, have the power to transport us to times and places from our past. If you're like me, a good percentage of your teen years were spent slathering your body with coconut lotion poolside or at the beach. Put those memories to work for you now! Smooth on some lotion, get horizontal in your favorite hammock or lounge chair, close your eyes, and you'll practically hear the sound of the waves and the gulls.

Paper umbrellas. Pop one in your glass of lemonade, your bottle of Evian water, or your can of Sprite. Whatever you're drinking will take on a festive air with the colorful touch of one of these vacation icons. And while you're at it, dig out the plastic lei from your daughter's dress-up box and slip it around your neck. If, after all that, you get the urge to dance the hula, go right ahead — just make sure the neighbors don't see you.

Flowers. This spring, brighten your backyard with some colorful blooms. Even a few pots of bright flowers, strategically placed around your getaway spot, will help transform your patio or yard. Create pockets of beauty that can provide visual pleasure the next time you need a distraction from stress, yet don't have time to travel farther than your own backyard.

Visit a Foreign Country

If you don't want to take a vacation in your backyard, you could always take three hours and visit a foreign country!

This is a fun one to do with your family. Select a country. Some place in Asia might be nice. Or how about Mexico or Spain? Visit a local travel agency and peruse brochures that tell about the country you've selected. Then drive to your public library. Spend an hour looking at books and magazines related to your country. Look for a picture of the flag. Find something that talks about national holidays or costumes. Find a picture book of the landscape.

Many libraries have computers with access to the Internet. You can probably find lots of information about your country on the World Wide Web. And while you're there, check out the tape library. It's possible that your library may have on hand an audiotape featuring music or language lessons for the country you have chosen. If so, listen to it in the car as you continue your trip.

Now for something a little more experiential. Is there a district or market in your city that caters to immigrants from the country you are "visiting"? When I lived in California, Alvera Street was twenty minutes from my home, offering sights and sounds and tastes that celebrated a Hispanic heritage. Near my house now there is a wonderful Asian market. Walking the aisles, I am exposed to unfamiliar sights and smells. I can buy a Chinese newspaper, look at product labels in Chinese, see and smell unknown spices, purchase samples of unfamiliar snacks and candies, and sometimes even hear unfamiliar languages.

Depending on the time of day and the country you are "visiting," you might even be able to attend a worship service. Many Korean churches shared church facilities with English-speaking congregations near our California home. It was easy to find Korean-speaking congregations holding worship services on Saturday afternoon or evening.

Finally, take your family to dinner. Select a restaurant that serves the cuisine of the country you've chosen. Chinese, Mexican, Indian, Thai, French . . . a cruise through the *Yellow Pages* should reveal a number of choices!

Take a Sixty-Second Vacation!

Sometimes we don't have three hours to enjoy international culture, or even forty-five minutes to swing in the hammock in the backyard. For times like these, we might be well served by a micro-minivacation. That's right! In sixty seconds or less, we can get away from it all without even leaving the building!

Advertising executive Manning Rubin has written a fun little book entitled *60 Ways to Relieve Stress in 60 Seconds* (Workman, 1993).

Of course, some folks scoff at the idea that a minute is long enough to do anyone any good. And yet, as Mr. Rubin points out: "Try waiting a full minute after you ask someone to pass the cream for your coffee, especially if it's the first cup of the day. Or count slowly all the way to sixty and see how much time goes by. The truth is, a minute is a long time — certainly long enough to calm yourself down if you use it properly." Rubin promises his sixty-second "vacations" can help us reduce and control the effects of stress. You should order the book and try them all. But in the meantime, shall we sample a few? Here are some of my favorites:

Take a moment from whatever stress-producing activity you are currently engaged in and . . .

. . . try to draw a nearby object — a chair, a plant, your computer.

. . . drink a glass of water in exactly thirty sips.

. . . try to recall the contents of your pockets or purse. Write down as many items as you can.

. . . guess how many steps it will take to walk to a spot nearby — the coffee machine, bathroom, or front door. Then walk there and see how close you came.

. . . make yourself laugh out loud.

Think of something funny to get
yourself started.

. . . give your pet a sixty-second
scratch.

. . . listen to the sound of something
nearby — the air conditioner,
traffic, or anything else. Close
your eyes and turn it into a
soothing sound.

. . . close your eyes and try to draw a
perfect circle.

Home-Based Vacation

Surely you've noticed the trend. It
started twenty years ago when people
began looking for more opportunities to
work from their own homes. Now
telecommuting is big business. And it
hasn't stopped there! The Home Shopping
Club means I can shop from my home.
Closed-circuit TV means I can go to
school from my home. The Internet means
I can browse the Library of Congress from
my home. My supermarket just launched a
program where I can buy groceries from
my home.

I figured it was only a matter of time
until someone came up with the home-

based vacation. So I decided it should be me.

Now, what I'm about to describe is a bit more than a "mini-vacation," but it's flexible and convenient enough that I thought it was worth mentioning. Our home-based vacation is going to take place over four days, but you could just as easily coordinate one to take place over two days, or even one.

But I'm getting ahead of myself! Let me explain how this idea came about:

Next week is spring vacation. Kaitlyn is out of school. Larry even took some vacation time so we could do something fun as a family. Among the ideas that were batted about was renting a beachfront motel room in Galveston. I was thrilled. We could even go horseback riding on the beach. Larry, however, said the room would cost so much we couldn't afford any actual entertainment while we were there. I said we could stay up late and watch cable and play Monopoly. Larry reminded me we would be sharing a room with a two-year-old, meaning we could either (a) all go to bed at 8:30, or (b) let Kacie stay up way past her bedtime and go ahead and pay for the damages to the room when we checked out.

That's when I came up with the idea to just stay home. For four days we're going to take day-trips with our kids. The zoo is on our agenda, as well as children's museums, bowling, a train ride, and even a movie. We'll be home in time for naps. We can sleep in our own beds. And, on top of all that, Larry and I are going to take the money we would have spent on the motel, hire a baby-sitter every night, and enjoy dinner and a movie on our own!

What a deal — something for everyone! A vacation like this accommodates busy schedules, different tastes, vast chasms in age groups, and can be tailored for nearly any length of time.

Best of all, it doesn't require a TripTik or include the words "jet lag," "Are we there yet?" or "But I didn't have to go when we were still at the hotel!"

Become a Time Traveler

Want a minivacation that's almost as fun as it was the first time around? Try becoming a time traveler — and still be home in time to pick up the kids from school. How? Fix something hot to drink, curl up in a quiet, comfortable spot, and break out the photo albums.

Go all the way back. Baby pictures? How about that shot of you dancing naked in your crib? Look, there you are on the first day of school. Here's one . . . must have been Halloween . . . oops! Sorry. I guess that was the style back then. Prom photos, wedding photos . . . that attractive shot of you in a hospital gown, looking like you just got run over by a Mac truck yet beaming nonetheless as you hold your firstborn child . . .

My photo albums are fine, but the real treasure trove is the cardboard box our computer came in. I started storing a few photos in there until I found time to put them in an album. Now the box holds nearly a decade of memories and requires four men and an act of Congress to move it from room to room.

I went through the box a couple of weeks ago. Actually, Kaitlyn and I spent an hour poring over photos, kindergarten master-pieces, and yellowed birthday cards. We had reached the bottom of the box when the phone rang. Phone? Wait . . . where was I? Looking around my living room, it took a moment for the memories to fall away and for me to place myself back soundly in the present. What time was it anyway? How long had we been gone . . . I mean busy?

Take a trip down memory lane. You'll not only enjoy a diversion from current stress, but you'll also come away with a whole new perspective. Reliving those fond Kodak moments — and being reminded, at the same time, just how fast time flies! — may very well leave you with a new commitment to enjoy and cherish the time you have with your family today.

A Friend in Need Needs a Friend, Indeed

I'll never forget the day I made The Phone Call.

Stressed out by an overabundance of diapers, deadlines, and dirty dishes in my life, I was feeling under siege. Anxious. Overwhelmed. And so, looking for comfort, I did the only thing I could think of at the moment.

I went to the kitchen.

Ten minutes later I picked up the phone and dialed the phone number of bosom buddy Linda Holland. As soon as she answered, I found myself blurting my woes into the receiver.

"Help!" I cried. "I've just eaten an entire box of Cap'n Crunch!"

I knew my friend was a kindred spirit —

a sympathetic soul who had "been there, done that" — when she immediately answered, "Ouch! Do you know what that'll do to the roof of your mouth?"

How did she know? Firsthand experience, no doubt.

When life gets a little rough, Cap'n Crunch is a stopgap measure. A temporary fix. A short-term solution. Chocolate is another short-term solution. Now I'll be the first to admit that eating chocolate doesn't produce lacerations on the roof of your mouth like an entire box of Cap'n Crunch has been known to do, but eating chocolate has its own set of disparaging side effects. Just ask my bathroom scale. On second thought, don't ask my scale. It has been privy to dark secrets even my husband will never know, and I'd just as soon keep it that way.

My point is that there are plenty of quick fixes around, things we can do that make us feel better for, oh, about a nano-second until guilt or regret sets in. And those post-binge pounds aren't exactly a picnic, either.

And yet, in a world of quick fixes, we have alternatives. I'd like to talk about one of those alternatives in particular. It lasts longer than a box of Milk Duds. Nourishes better than a Twinkie. Has less calories than a Milky Way Lite. And is easier on the palate than Cap'n Crunch.

It's called friendship.

When we're feeling stressed, we tend to reach for the food. Maybe we should reach for the phone instead.

Button, Button, Who's Got the Button?

I've been blessed with some really wonderful friends. You and I have lots of people in our lives, don't we? Colleagues, acquaintances, neighbors . . . people who share our pew, carpool our kids, and type memos for our husbands. But every now and then someone crosses the line. They stop being an acquaintance or colleague and become a true friend.

When do you know someone has graduated to the status of being a true friend?

- When she can show up on your doorstep unannounced and your first thought isn't about yesterday's breakfast dishes in your kitchen sink.
- When you can stop in the middle of a

sentence and say, "Am I whining?" and she knows you well enough to say "Yes."

- When you come home from work and find a note on your kitchen counter that says, "Couldn't find my can opener, so I let myself in and borrowed yours."
- When she says, "How are you doing?" and you know she really wants to know.
- When she'll tell you about the lipstick on your teeth or spinach at your gum line.

I think my friend Nancy Rottmeyer crossed a line into new friendship territory the day she came over and helped me paint and wallpaper my kitchen. The significance of this act of friendship takes on new meaning when you realize that Nancy and her husband, Larry, had just finished *paying professionals* to paint and wallpaper several rooms in their home. Trust me when I say that this fact did not go unnoticed by Nancy's husband when our two families met for pizza that night. His tongue-in-cheek observation ("Let me get this straight. Wallpapering *our* house was too much work, but you wallpapered

Karen's kitchen *just for fun?*") made me appreciate Nancy's assistance all the more.

My friend Cherie Spurlock drops in for a visit, whips up some soapy water, and does my dishes while we chat. I called her house the other night at ten thirty, desperate for a blank videotape for a project I needed to finish before morning. After looking around, she came back on the line and said casually, "Nope. I don't have one. But tell me what kind you need and I'll run down to the supermarket and pick something up." I was moved by her generous offer, but told her I couldn't let her do that. Then she volunteered the services of her seventeen-year-old son. Now there was an offer I couldn't refuse!

How do you know someone's a true friend? There's something about that "extra" mile that says volumes. Yet sometimes it's not so much what a friend *does* as what she *perceives*.

When I became pregnant with Kacie, I had a hard time feeling any joy or excitement about my pregnancy, despite the fact that it was a long-awaited event. I know that my caution stemmed from a miscarriage several years earlier. What if I lost this baby, too? Maybe it was safer to postpone my excitement several months, until I could be certain this baby would survive.

That's when a bouquet of spring flowers arrived at my door. The note, penned by my friend Linda Holland, said, "Celebrate the new life within you!" And somehow, after her encouragement, I could.

Occasionally, however, something happens in a friendship that defies categorization. All you know for sure is that a mere acquaintance never would have risen to the occasion.

Like the day I went shopping with Beth Forester. The treasure I sought was a fancy blouse to wear to a glamorous dinner. Before long, I found the perfect blouse. And it was on clearance, too! The only problem was that it was missing two buttons.

Beth and I were standing together in my dressing room when she picked up an identical blouse, also on clearance, draped over a chair. "What's wrong with this one? It's not missing any buttons."

I sighed. "Wrong size."

And then we had an idea. As long as the store was going to have to sell a blouse with missing buttons, why shouldn't it be the blouse that didn't fit me? At my inquiry, an apathetic shrug from the dressing room attendant gave us the permission we needed. The problem was, we didn't have a pair of scissors or clippers with which to snip two buttons from the too-small blouse.

Beth raised the blouse to her teeth.

"There's one," she spit into her hand.

For the second button she resorted to her keys. She soon discovered that Buick keys saw through thread faster than keys associated with, say, Saturns or Chevys.

I wore my blouse the next evening. And what an evening it was! One of my books was up for an award, and I felt gorgeous and confident in my new outfit. And even though the Gold Medallion went to someone else, the evening was magical. *Pillow Talk* was one of five finalists in its category. The music was heavenly. The speaker, dynamic. The food, rich and sumptuous.

That was eight months ago. This morning I walked into my closet and spotted the blouse I wore to the banquet. And when I did, the memories came flooding back, and I had to laugh.

You see, whenever I see that blouse, the thoughts that come to mind are not of candlelight and glory. Nah. I think of Beth, standing in the women's dressing room, biting the buttons off a clearance-rack treasure.

Now, *that's* a true friend.

Becoming a Better Friend

I want to be a good friend to my friends.

Unfortunately, sometimes I miss birthdays or forget to return a phone call. Occasionally I show up late when I'm meeting a pal for lunch, and my house is neither spic nor span when friends come over to chat.

Luckily, my friends know me pretty well. They understand that my memory's not worth a wooden nickel . . . that the only way I arrive anywhere on time is when I forget to set my clock back in the fall . . . that my house has piles that would impress even the folks who make Preparation H. Yet I think they also know that my intentions are good. Friendships are important to me. I cherish the women who enrich my life with their quirky personalities, quick wit, and seasoned wisdom.

Still, I know I could be a better friend. It's possible you feel the same way, too. What can we do, you and I, to sharpen our skills in the friendship department? How can we become better friends to our friends?

I asked six women to tell me what they valued in a friendship. I've consolidated their answers in a list that I call "Dos and Don'ts

60

of Feminine Fellowship." Here goes:

Do Follow Up on Promises

If you tell a friend you'll pray for her, really do it! In fact, dropping your friend a postcard in the mail on the day you remember her in prayer might be just the encouragement she needs!

Do Learn the Art of Listening

Body language says a lot. Are you listening with your eyes as well as your ears? Also, make sure you don't respond to every comment by saying, "You know, the exact same thing happened to me," and turning the conversation to your issues. Instead, ask follow-up questions to learn more about your friend and her situation, and demonstrate interest in what she's telling you.

Do Celebrate Your Friend's Happiness and Success

Did your friend just get a promotion at

work? Find out she's pregnant? Lose fifteen pounds? Let her know you're thrilled when she experiences the good things life has to offer. If you let jealousy or competition keep you from celebrating with your friends, you may find yourself alone, with no one who cares about your good news when the tide turns and your ship comes in.

Do Love Your Friend Enough to Tell Her the Truth

If a friend asks you if a bathing suit makes her look like a boat, you might want to refrain from asking if she means houseboat or cruise ship. At the same time, if the suit she's picked is the least flattering of the bunch, she'll appreciate your diplomatic attempt to steer her toward a better option.

It's tempting to want to tell people what we think they want to hear, but the very best friends care enough to tell the truth. Do I have lipstick on my teeth? Yes. I had this big fight with my husband last night — do you think I overreacted and should apologize? *From what you told me, you definitely owe him dinner and roses.* Does this dress make me look fat? *You've got a nice waistline. Let's see if we can find something that shows it off better.* You get the idea.

Do Be an Encourager

Beyond our front doors, life's a jungle. It can be a jungle this side of the front door too. You know what can make all the difference in the world? An encouraging word from someone who really cares about us. Did your friend tell you she wants to lose weight? Improve her marriage? Stop smoking? Get her head on straight? Reorganize her pantry? Beat breast cancer? Survive this divorce? Climb out of her depression? Get on track with God?

Let her know you believe in her.

The words "You can do this" mean a lot.

The words "I'll be there to encourage you any way I can" mean even more.

And the phrase "You know, it's Jesus who can give us the strength to accomplish even the toughest things in life — I'll be praying for your relationship with him" might mean the most of all.

Don't Hide behind a Facade of Perfection or Control

Vulnerability says a lot. Do you trust your friend enough to tell her the truth about struggles or imperfections in your life? If not, she probably won't feel comfortable confiding in you either.

Don't Tell Secrets!

Mum's the word. If a friend shares something confidential, don't disclose her secret — no matter how juicy it is!

Don't Try to Have an Answer for Everything

Sometimes, in the face of a friend's deep pain, there are no answers that will suffice. Holding a hand, hugging a shoulder, or shedding tears together may be better options.

Wanted: A Shoulder to Cry On

We all want to be better friends. And yet, sometimes the thing we want most of all is someone who can be a good friend to us.

I know when I'm hurting or struggling, there are certain friends I can count on as sources of great comfort. These friends have seen me at my best and my worst. I can tell them anything (and just about have) with full confidence that even the most sordid confession will not cause them to waver in their love for me. The individuals who fall into this category are not judgmental or critical of my shortcomings. As a general rule, they don't usually offer pat answers or microwave solutions. Instead, they encourage me, hold me accountable, give me passionate advice that I occasionally follow, and laugh and cry with me.

Now, I'll be the first to admit that friends like this are hard to find. And yet it's worth the effort to cultivate friendships like these.

When the name of the game is pain, sometimes we just need someone to talk to.

Yet how do we choose that person? If we don't have a history with friends we know we can trust, how do we decide with whom we can open up? How can we be fairly confident that the person to whom we are baring our very souls will not recoil in horror, blush with embarrassment, shake a shaming finger, or give dangerous advice in answer to our dilemma?

Looking for someone in whom you can confide? Here's a checklist of characteristics you might want to consider:

Choose someone who has been vulnerable and transparent with you. If you have a friend who has never let you past her facade of perfection, you might want to think twice before blurting out your deepest and darkest secrets over a hamburger and fries. If a friend is uncomfortable with her own imperfections and struggles, she probably won't have a clue how to respond appropriately to yours.

How important is mutual vulnerability and transparency? Psychotherapist Novlyn Hinson says, "Sometimes, if I am faced with a client who is struggling to open up and talk about her issues, I'll drop my guard a little. I'll share something from my own life. As I become transparent, I've entrusted her with something intimate from my own life. She may feel, in turn, that I can be trusted with her transparency as well."

I do this in my friendships at times. If I sense that a friend is burdened about something — but seems hesitant to talk to me about it — I'll look for an opportunity to share something personal of my own. It sounds manipulative, and I guess it could be if the message I am sending by my transparency were a lie. But it's not. By my transparency I am saying — with all sincerity — "Our friendship is a safe place in which to share burdens. I can trust you with this personal part of my life . . . and you can trust me too."

Choose someone who practices confidentiality. I know a woman who brims with entertaining tales from the lives of other people, some of whom I know, most of whom I have never met. There is nothing malicious in her stories — she just can't keep a secret.

One night Larry and I were driving home from an evening spent with this woman and her husband, when Larry spoke the words that were on my mind as well: "Gee, I wonder if she talks about us behind our backs?"

Good question. Don't set yourself up for disillusionment, embarrassment, and even bitterness by sharing sensitive details of your life with friends who haven't mastered the art of discretion! By the same token, when someone shares something sensitive with you, remember the golden rule and treat her secret as if it were your own.

Choose someone who shares your values and strives to make wise choices. If one of your girlfriends has dumped her last four husbands because they left the toilet seat up, you might want to think twice before seeking her advice about your marital woes. The point is to confide in someone who is capable of giving you wise encouragement and advice in line with your personal convictions.

It's okay to choose someone who has experienced the kind of pain or struggle with which you are wrestling. I have a couple of friends who have experienced depression, as I have. When I feel myself slipping back toward the abyss that claimed my life for several years, I know I can rely on these women to be ardent encouragers. Do they have all the answers? No way. Sometimes they still struggle too. But I know they've walked a similar path, and whatever answers they may have gleaned will be shared with me in a heartbeat.

I have to admit, though, I don't go to these friends for their answers. I go to them for the passion I see in their faces when they look me in the eyes and say, "I know you're tired. But please hang on. You can get through this."

Sometimes we strategize together. What changes can we make in our lives that will lift our spirits and help us cope? Sometimes we pray together. Sometimes we hold each other accountable. When one friend felt herself losing ground, she admitted she needed to make an appointment with the counselor she hadn't seen in a year, but kept putting off making the call. I gave her a deadline of four days: "I'm calling you Friday morning to make sure you've made your appointment. And if you haven't, I'm coming over and sitting in your living room until you do." She made the call.

Several months later, I told her I was feeling overwhelmed with housework and needed desperately to hire a housekeeper to come in for one day and help me crawl out from under the piles. When I never made the call — just kept complaining about my situation — well, you can guess what she said to me.

I missed the deadline by one day. But I made the call and got the help I needed.

Accountability coming from someone who seems to have her life completely "together" can feel stifling and obtrusive. Accountability coming from a friend who has scars and wounds of her own is both humbling and empowering.

Who Ya Gonna Call?

Want the number of a good stress-buster? My guess is that there is a phone number — in fact you may even know it by heart — of someone in your life who can help lighten your load. When we're hurting, our first inclination may be to withdraw from life and lick our wounds. And yet isolation rarely is the answer.

Reach out to a friend. It would be nice if our friends were mind readers who knew instinctively when we needed an encouraging word. Unfortunately, they usually need us to clue them in.

Don't be shy. Call a friend. Let her know you're stressed or hurting or confused. Receive the comfort your friend has to give. Then, when your spirits have been lifted even a little, celebrate with some festive refreshment.

Cap'n Crunch always works for me.

Sometimes it's hard to admit vulnerability, even to a close friend. Here are some things you can say to break the ice:

"I'm discouraged about something. Maybe you can help me see things in a new light."

"I'm so stressed by things going on in my life right now, a tax audit would feel like a vacation."

"Put on your counseling hat. I need someone to talk to about something."

"Is your shoulder water-proof?"

"Remember the kids' book entitled *Alexander and the Terrible, Horrible, No Good, Very Bad Day*? Well, you can call me Alexander because I'm having one of those days."

When a friend is really hurting, sometimes words fall short. Here are some things you can do to demonstrate your empathy when a friend is really blue and needs her spirits lifted:

Take your friend a pot filled with soil and flower bulbs. Seeing the rejuvenating power of nature at work can sometimes lift a troubled spirit.

Did you pray for your friend this week? Grab a piece of paper, pen the words "Dear Lord," and begin writing, word for word, your prayer for your friend. Give it to her as a tangible representation of the intangible power of prayer.

Give a gift that caters to one of the five senses: an oven-fresh batch of cookies, a compact disc filled with praise songs or soothing instrumentals, a packet of simmering potpourri, a cotton throw. A troubled heart may not yet be able to assimilate the comfort offered by words, philosophies, and theories. Sometimes, when we're in deep pain, our first line of defense may be found in more primitive, sensory forms of comfort: a warm blanket, a quiet and dark room, beautiful music, the serenity of a sunset, a hot cup of tea, or a home-baked cookie. Now don't get me wrong. I'm not suggesting that a cup of Lipton's and a Toll House cookie can mend a broken heart. But sometimes, soothing the senses can provide a temporary balm until the head and heart can handle the tougher job of working through pain.

4

Would You Like a Little Cheese with Your Whine?

Ever feel like whining?

I just got home from the supermarket. If anything makes me want to pull up a chair and whine, it's looking in the refrigerator and realizing I'm going to have to spend the next forty minutes getting intimate with last month's leftovers if I'm going to have a shot at getting this week's milk and eggs in cold storage.

In my book *Happily Ever After . . . And 21 Other Myths about Family Life*, I wrote about having refrigerator leftovers that have been around so long they're starting to get their own junk mail. Unfortunately, at this particular moment my leftovers have evolved beyond the junk mail stage and are approaching higher intelligence. Forget the Lillian Vernon catalog. I looked in there today and found last year's tuna casserole reading the *Wall Street Journal*.

I always know when it's time to clean out my refrigerator. It's time to clean out the fridge when I run out of Tupperware. I remember one time I cleaned out my refrigerator and ended up with so much Tupperware I got the hostess gift *plus* the stacking sandwich caddies.

Of course, one of the downsides of keeping leftovers around too long is that, at some point (and you're never quite sure exactly when this point occurs), the edible becomes inedible. I get very stressed if I have to leave town on business for a couple of days, because I can't be certain my family fully understands the need to use discretion while looking for a quick meal. I know this is hard to believe, but they actually think they can just open the refrigerator door at any given moment and choose, willy-nilly, from among the options. They don't understand that choosing a leftover from the refrigerator at our house is a little like playing Russian Roulette. That's why I always look tired if I am flying out of town for a speaking engagement or book tour. It's not because my flight left at 7:00 A.M. It's because I stayed up until 3:00 A.M. cleaning out the refrigerator so no one dies of food poisoning while I'm away.

So far there have been no actual casualties. There are no notches on my refrigerator door. Close calls, however, are another story.

One morning I slept in. I was dead tired, having spent half the night nursing a two-year-old with a stuffy nose. As a result, my husband woke our eleven-year-old and helped her get ready for school. Since the school cafeteria was closed that week, he even made a sack lunch for her.

About ten that morning, Kacie and I sat down to breakfast. And suddenly I had a horrible thought.

I rushed to the phone and dialed Kaitlyn's school. I asked the puzzled secretary to pull Kaitlyn out of class and bring her to the phone. I told her it was an emergency.

"Mom?" Kaitlyn asked a moment later. "Everything okay?"

"Sweetie, Dad made your lunch this morning, right?"

"Right."

"He didn't happen to make you a ham sandwich, did he?"

"Yeah, he did."

"Don't eat it."

"Don't eat it?"

"Not unless you happen to have a stomach pump on hand. What time does your class break for lunch?"

"11:30."

"I'll be there."

I swung through McDonald's for a Happy Meal. That afternoon I threw out the ham. It had been there since last spring. It wasn't as evolved as the tuna, though. It was only reading the *TV Guide*.

Whiners Anonymous

Am I the only woman who can spend twenty minutes whining about something as insignificant as the management of refrigerator leftovers?

And that's not even my forte. Bad hair days, broken nails, PMS, feeling overcommitted, last night's argument with my husband . . . I can whine about it all. You might call me, in fact, a connoisseur of fine whine.

But just because you and I know how to whine doesn't mean we feel good about doing it, right? You know what I'm talking about. Friends call us on the phone and say, "How are you doing?" and we're embarrassed to tell the truth. The truth is that we feel stressed, anxious, overwhelmed, and we have this strong urge to whine . . . but we feel foolish doing it because there's nothing seriously wrong with our lives.

Oh, don't get me wrong. Neither you nor I live storybook lives. There are plenty of times we've faced serious problems and even tragedy. But sometimes, even when everything is going relatively right, we still manage to find things to complain about, don't we?

Is that okay? Are there any benefits to be derived from a fine whine now and then? What about whining etiquette? Are there rules that can help us get the most from a good whine without driving away our closest friends? And what about social whining? Is it okay to whine and dine with friends, or are we better off keeping our complaints to ourselves? And even if we happen to decide that a little whine now and then is good for the heart, what about excessive whining? If we realize we're crossing the line, how can we change our patterns and adopt healthier responses?

Define Whine

I raised these questions and more this morning during a breakfast get-together with three girlfriends. A couple months ago Darla Talley, Nancy Rottmeyer, Cherie Spurlock, and I stumbled into the pleasant tradition of meeting every Friday morning for breakfast at a Cracker Barrel near our homes. This morning, I had barely sat down when Darla said to the other women: "Hmmm. Yellow legal pad and a pen behind her ear. She's working on a chapter and wants to brainstorm."

I conceded with a sheepish grin. "Okay, so I lack mystery."

Over hash browns and fried apples, one of the things we decided was that whining is different than being assertive. We talked about the time Darla and her husband went to a nice restaurant for some intimate conversation — and found themselves in a crowded dining section. They asked for a quieter table. Actually, they had to ask twice, but in the end their need was met. Darla wondered if they had been whiney. We chewed on that one a few minutes, then concluded what the Talleys had been in that situation was *assertive*, which can be a very healthy thing.

It's okay to verbalize a need or want. It's called communication. It's a valuable tool.

Of course, we can cross the line, which leads us to the following question: When exactly does communication turn into whining?

If you're not sure, this may help. Here are some telltale signs that you are, indeed, engaged in a verifiable whine:

If you find yourself using the same annoying tone your children used last week just before you flew off the handle and sent them to their rooms for a month . . .

If your complaint becomes repetitive and ceases any chance of being productive . . .

If you don't even *care* whether your complaint is productive — just repeating it over and over feels really good . . .

If someone offers a solution to your dilemma and brings your pity party to a premature halt, ruining your entire day . . .

If your best friend starts wearing a

T-shirt that says, "I'm sorry, you must have mistaken me for your therapist" . . .

If a colleague overhears you talking in your office . . . and mistakes your voice for the fax machine . . .

If your friends and family know the details of your sad stories better than you do . . .

If your therapist asks if you have a quarter, then politely tells you to call someone who cares . . .

If, next to you, Rodney Dangerfield is beginning to look like an optimist . . .

then there's a good chance you're whining!

Whining? You're in Good Company. But Here's How to Stop Anyway

What do you get when you whine? Well, sometimes you actually get what you want. That's not such a bad deal, right? Of course, in the process you may very well compromise your personal dignity, circumvent healthier channels of communication, provide a poor example for your children to mimic, and basically annoy the heck out of anyone within earshot. But other than that, I guess you could call whining an effective communication technique.

I don't mean to lay a guilt trip. We all whine now and then. It's an unalienable right. I think it's even in the constitution, somewhere between eating chocolate and reading *Good Housekeeping* in the bathroom.

Still, what if we had some alternatives? What if we began looking at some other options that might prove more efficient and beneficial than whining? With these questions in mind, I've compiled six "Whine Busters" designed to help us do one of two things: (a) decline the whine (Yes, it really is possible to replace the whine with new attitudes, new actions, and new communication), or (b) refine the whine (for those times we fall off the wagon and decide to indulge in a little whine after all). Are there good habits, boundaries, and principles that can make our whining more productive than destructive? You bet. And here they are:

1. Look on the bright side. Sometimes I'm in mid-whine when I have a burst of insight that stops me cold in my tracks. And that insight is this: I realize I'm looking at the glass as half empty when there is clearly another option.

I'm prone to whine about my workload when I take on too many projects. And yet, as a writer and speaker, I WANT to be in demand. When my calendar fills up with speaking engagements, radio interviews, and deadlines for articles and books, guess what? THAT MEANS I'M EXPERIENCING SUCCESS IN MY CHOSEN FIELD. Do I really want to whine about success? I don't think so.

What about your whine? Is there a bright side somewhere that you're overlooking?

2. Count your blessings. Some days it feels as though everything is going wrong as dozens of small frustrations converge on me all at the same time. I open my mail and discover I was a day late making my deposit and now I've bounced a check. Then my computer crashes and I lose all the work I've done since lunch. Running late to pick up kids from school, I get in the car and discover the gas needle hovering on "E." I set off the smoke alarm while cooking dinner, and the contractor calls and tells me that in order to repair the garage door I backed into last week, he will have to charge me a sum roughly equivalent to the amount Bill Clinton paid in lawyer fees during his term in office. By the end of the day, it's easy to focus on what's going wrong in my life and lose sight of all that's going right.

You know, the Bible tell us "whatsoever things are pure, whatsoever things are right . . . think on these things." Well, why not? Stop complaining. Look at your watch. For one minute do nothing but name the positive things happening in your life:

"My kids are healthy."

"My husband and I saw a really funny movie last week."

"My mother-in-law sent me a really sweet greeting card."

"We've got a roof over our heads and food to eat."

"My daughter makes good grades, and I'm thrilled at her success."

"My toddler says the funniest things. She makes me laugh every day!"

"My husband loves his job!"

One full minute. And don't cheat.

Count your blessings. An old-fashioned idea, but a great way nonetheless to change your perspective and lift your spirits.

3. *Practice courage and serenity.* Remember this prayer? "Lord, grant me the courage to change what I can, and the serenity to accept what I cannot." If you can be an agent for change by giving voice to problems and injustice, then have at it. Be courageous. Be assertive. Like Mike and Darla at the steak house, make a request. Make it more than once if you have to. But do it with respect for yourself and your listener.

On the other hand, if something is beyond your control, accept what you can. Be gracious. If you need to express disappointment, do so in a voice that doesn't sound like a fax machine.

Courage. Serenity. Two sides of the same coin. Practice them both.

4. *Confine the whine.* What if we look on the bright side, count our blessings, practice courage and serenity, and we still feel like whining?

The fact is, sometimes whining makes us feel better. And who knows? Maybe in some circumstances, there's something therapeutic about making a mountain out of a molehill. But perhaps the key is moderation. While long-term whining is destructive to our outlook, our spirits, and our relationships, a short-term whine may well provide an outlet without doing too much damage in the process!

How can you confine the whine? Call a good friend or your spouse ("Hi, it's me . . ."). Define the parameters at the beginning ("I'm having a bad day and I need to whine about it. Would you do me a favor and just listen to me whine?"). Set a time limit ("Ten minutes, tops"). Then whine away.

When you're done, find a way to laugh about the experience. You might say, "I feel so much better now. What do I owe you, doctor?" Or maybe: "I'm done. Am I a good whiner? On a scale from 1 to 10, how'd I do?"

You're not only confining the whine to a limited time, but you're also getting a chuckle out of the experience, which does wonders just by itself. Even the Bible, after all, concedes that a merry heart is good medicine! The goal is to not take yourself too seriously. Whining is fine, but whining with your tongue in your cheek is even better.

5. *Look for a solution.* If I'm in the mood to whine, the last thing I want my husband to do is solve my problem right away. The thing I REALLY need for him to do is just hear me out. Then, after five or ten minutes as I begin to lose steam, I'm more open to a good solution!

At some point during the whining experience, turn the table. Move away from the complaint and toward a constructive response. Brainstorm. Come up with creative solutions. From that conversation, put one constructive idea into action this week.

6. *Don't whine about privilege.* Finally, if we're going to go ahead and whine anyway, we should remember this cruel fact of life: Even our closest friends will have a hard time tolerating our moans and groans about things that many women would consider blessings. For example, stop whining pitifully about the ten disfiguring pounds that are absolutely ruining your life, particularly if the friend listening to you tops her scale at 220 pounds and would give her eyeteeth to have the figure you despise.

Stop moaning and groaning about all the taxes you're having to pay now that your husband's promotion doubled his salary. If you are remodeling your summer home and the interior designer just told you the $90-per-yard drapery fabric you love is on back order, don't look for sympathy from your colleague who scrimped for six years to buy a 900-square-foot bungalow with avocado linoleum and Stone Age plumbing.

I once went to lunch with my mom and two sisters where, over chicken salad and iced tea, my sister Renee filled us in on her dating woes. Finding the right man, she moaned, wasn't easy to do . . . especially when so many men seemed so pushy when it came to physical intimacy! The rest of us commiserated with Renee. We were there for her. We gave her our unending sympathy.

And then she blew it.

With sincere frustration in her voice, she said: "You have no idea how it feels to be attractive and have men want you all the time!"

Now, I'll admit that Renee is gorgeous. She's got a mane of thick black hair, long legs, and more. And I know she didn't mean for her comment to come out the way it did! But it was sort of hard to sympathize with her after that. We all got a good laugh out of it, sure, but in the end, we decided hers was a pretty flattering problem to have.

So here's the bottom line.

If you're five pounds away from a size 9 . . .

If you've got too much money, too many admirers, or your husband won't stop bringing you flowers no matter HOW often you beg . . .

If your teenagers are so well behaved you feel left out when other mothers talk about their parenting dilemmas . . .

If your husband wants to take you to the south of France and you *don't* have a *thing* to wear . . .

If you get carded every time you buy a bottle of cooking wine at the grocery store, or acquaintances keep mistaking you for your daughter's *younger* sister . . .

Don't come whining to me. Because I'll only have one thing to say: Just grin and bear it.

Here's the Story of a Man Named Brady . . .

Love can give your heart wings. Of course, it can also give you heartburn. My friend Diane was closer to the heartburn stage as she sat at my kitchen table and spilled her tale of woe.

She was dating a man who was madly in love with her. He often talked about their future together, about the kids they would have, about the life they would build, and even about the kind of wedding ceremony they would have.

There was just one small element missing from this happy picture: a marriage proposal.

"Why hasn't he proposed?" Diane whined.

I didn't have a solution. What I did have

was a bag of Oreo cookies, which of course is the next best thing.

Diane and I talked about her dilemma while eating the middles out of our cookies. We rehashed how Diane and Hector had met and how long they'd been together. We analyzed educational status, career developments, family responsibilities — anything that could possibly have a bearing on Hector's apparent marriage proposal disability. And then an hour or so into our pity party, we made The Discovery. It changed everything. It gave us new perspective. It brought sanity and sense to the situation. Suddenly, everything was so much clearer.

It started when one of us — I don't remember who — looked thoughtfully into the distance and said, "Bet you can't sing all three stanzas of the *Brady Bunch* theme song."

Maybe it was the lateness of the hour. Maybe we had run out of things to analyze regarding Hector and were ready to tackle a dilemma we actually had a shot at solving. Or maybe we'd just had a few too many Oreo cookies and the sugar and caffeine had severely impaired our judgment.

Whatever the reason, Diane sang out, "Here's the story of a lovely lady . . ."

I chimed in: "Who was bringing up three very lovely girls . . ."

"All of them had hair of gold, like their mother . . ."

"The youngest one in curls . . ."

Before we knew it, we had serenaded our way through the courtship of Mike and Carol Brady, belted out the theme to the *Beverly Hillbillies*, galloped through the *Mr. Ed* song, stumbled through an energetic rendition of all eight verses of *Gilligan's Island*, and sung several stanzas of "Doot doot doodoot doodoot doot," which any Nick-at-Nite fan will recognize as the theme song to *I Dream of Jeannie*.

By this time, let me assure you, we were no longer overly concerned with the length of time it was taking Hector to propose, nor whether Diane and Hector's first home together would be a condo at Retirement World. No, our biggest questions at that point had to do with the amount of money it must have taken to get Robert Reed to consent to that horrible perm, and whether or not Ginger and the Professor were secretly in love with each other.

Three weeks later, Hector proposed during an elaborate evening on the town. He said he'd been planning his proposal for months, but I'm not so sure. Diane and

I sang TV-land theme songs . . . and Hector proposed. You can't convince me that was just a coincidence. There's a connection somehow. In fact, I'd wager that, in the cosmic scheme of things, more things are wrought by TV-land theme songs than this world dreams of.

Sing Your Way to Better Mental Health

So what's the secret behind the therapeutic powers of old TV theme songs? How is it that belting out a song that begins, "Green Acres is the place for me . . ." can leave us feeling lighter and brighter than before we began singing? What would happen to road rage if we required every angry driver to sing one stanza from *Gilligan's Island* before cutting someone off in traffic, flashing the finger, or cocking a handgun? And what about stress-induced maladies? I'd wager that a group-sing of the theme from *The Monkees* could lower the blood pressure of even those with the most extreme Type-A tendencies.

Now, I wouldn't come right out and say that the American Medical Association is aware of the healing power of TV theme songs and is hiding this fact from the American public in an attempt to protect the financial bottom line of the entire medical industry, but the thought has crossed my mind.

Why is it that singing TV theme songs can make you feel better? I've got a couple of theories.

Distraction

First, it's distracting. It may take all your mental faculties and then some to remember the line that comes after "But they're cousins, identical cousins all the way" (from *The Patty Duke Show*). And while you're wrestling to recall the exact words and melody from a song you might not have heard in a couple of decades, guess what? There's a good chance your brain will be too busy to continue worrying about this month's credit card bill, next week's deadline, or last night's fight with your husband.

Is distraction a good long-term solution? Nah. But sometimes, as we're facing stress and dilemmas, what we can really use is a break. If we can get our minds off our problems for even a short while, we may find ourselves refreshed and our thinking clearer when we decide to tackle our problems again.

Intimate Fellowship

Another factor might be the healing dynamics that occur when we enjoy the fellowship of someone with whom we can drop our guard. Sure, you can sing TV theme songs by yourself, but why not double your pleasure (and your memory recall) by warbling with a friend? Of course, not just any friend will do. It has to be someone you don't have to impress, someone with whom you don't mind crossing the border into Sillyville, someone with whom you can laugh so hard you end up snorting through your nose and you don't even feel embarrassed.

And just being with that kind of a friend, well, there's something healing in that kind of fellowship, regardless of whether you're singing theme songs or sharing recipes or exchanging stories about your kids.

For a lot of us, the years we spent in Mayberry, or with the Cleavers, or on Gilligan's island were good years. Maybe we were newlyweds, or teens, or even kids. It may have seemed a kinder, gentler time in our lives. Certainly those were simpler years than we are experiencing today.

The mind is a miraculous thing. Memories are powerful. In fact, if we experienced something pleasurable twenty years ago, immersing ourselves in the memory of that event today may very well evoke familiar warm feelings. From my own experience, I know that sitting down to watch Gilligan's antics during my childhood was a pleasurable event. I was relaxed, happy to be home after a long day at school, ready to laugh. Recalling the theme song several decades later not only takes me back to those happy years, but can help me relive, in some fashion, good feelings from long ago.

Humor Helps

Finally, when we're feeling stressed or overwhelmed by the details of our lives,

How Well Do You Rate?

How well do you know your TV theme songs? Take this quiz and find out! Below are the first lines from ten TV theme songs. Do you know the name of each show? Better yet, can you sing any of the songs from start to finish? (You'll find the answers on the next page.)

1. "They're creepy and they're kooky"

2. "People let me tell you 'bout my best friend"

3. "Here we come, walking down the street"

4. "A horse is a horse, of course, of course"

5. "Diamonds, Daisies, Snow-flakes"

6. "Boy, the way Glen Miller played songs that made the hit parade"

7. "One, two, three, four, five, six, seven, eight"

8. "Love, exciting and new"

9. "Hello, world, here's a song

that we're singing.

10. "Welcome back, your dreams
were your ticket out"

what does it hurt to call to mind a few comic, slapstick images from the past? Remember Lucy as the Vita-vegimin gal? What about the Skipper in a grass skirt? And who can forget the cocky bumblings of Deputy Barney Fife!

As we hum the hallmark tunes, recalling funny characters and scenes from favorite shows can leave us smiling at the memory of their antics. And never, *never* underestimate the power of a smile. Indeed, humor is a powerful ally against the wounds of the world!

Life is tough. It can evoke emotions of frustration and anger and sadness. Of course, it can also evoke ecstasy and wonder and joy. The challenge lies in making the transition, in getting from here to there.

Good News for Memory-Challenged Crooners!

So what do you do if you can't remember the line that comes after Mr. Rogers' phrase, "It's a neighborly day in this beautywood" and it's driving you nuts? Copyright laws prevent me from printing the complete lyrics to the theme songs we all know and love. But don't despair! At the time this book went to press, I discovered a noteworthy web site with the lyrics of all of our favorites. Yes, all eight verses of the *Gilligan's Island* song are there, as well as lyrics for shows like *Dobie Gillis*, *The Brady Bunch*, and *Green Acres*. You'll even find the unaired words to the *Star Trek* theme! Check it out:

http://www.geocities.com/ Hollywood/Academy/4760/

The good news is that the gateway between frustration and happiness is often smaller than we think. We tend to think that, in order to even start the journey, we need an opening the size of a Mac truck. The fact is, sometimes to begin our journey, all we need is the smallest crack.

Crack a smile. If singing theme songs helps you do it, more power to you. The important thing is to find something silly and give in to the grin.

You'll be surprised at where you can go from there.

Sweet Dreams

Remember when we were kids? Remember all the big dreams we had? We were going to finance a swimming pool with the money we made selling lemonade in the front yard. We were going to grow up and become ballerinas, astronauts, and actresses. We actually believed we could talk our parents into buying us ponies for the backyard. We were going to emerge from puberty and look like Barbie.

Where did we go wrong?

Now don't misunderstand. I'm not lamenting the fact that you and I don't have Barbie-doll figures, nor am I grieving because we didn't actually become adolescent millionaires from peddling lemonade.

Okay, so maybe I am.

But that's not my point.

My point is that, now that we're grown-ups, what happened to our ability to dream the big dreams?

Let's face it. Grown-ups have wimpy goals.

You don't believe me? Let me just say that any goal that includes the words "dietary fiber" is a prime example of a wimpy goal.

We used to think we could fly to the moon. Now we're lucky if we can stay awake each evening long enough to watch *David Letterman*.

How Are Your Dreams Holding Up?

I'll be the first to admit that life can be tough on our big dreams. Even our wimpy dreams take a beating now and then.

And when we're depressed, feeling stress, or in the midst of PMS, any dream at all can seem frivolous. Indeed, it seems ridiculous to dream when all our energy is needed for more pressing endeavors like whining, yelling, crying, and generally feeling sorry for ourselves.

I remember when I was in the deepest part of my depression, before Larry and I had a complete understanding of the depth of my fall from sound thinking and healthy emotions. All we knew at that point was that something was terribly wrong.

I remember one evening in particular when Larry tried to reach me as I sat cocooned in numbness in the corner of the couch where I spent much of my time. He sat beside me and held me in his arms.

"I've been thinking," he said. "Remember how you always said you wanted to start a magazine? When we got married, it was all you talked about. You were so excited. You had it all planned out. I know I said at the time it would cost too much money and all, but I've been thinking, and I know you could do it. It would be worth the investment. What do you think?"

He searched my eyes for a glimmer of the dream that had once had the power to animate me for hours. It wasn't there.

I shook my head. "It just doesn't sound like fun anymore."

Nothing did. My tomorrows loomed pointless and empty. And the really scary part is that I didn't even care.

He tried all sorts of tactics to entice me back into the land of the living, dangling like a carrot all the dreams that had driven me in the past: book ideas and backyard Bible clubs, owning a horse and remodeling the house, publishing a magazine and learning to dance. Nothing lit a spark. He didn't realize that depression had eclipsed my dreams, leaving my world void of energy, light, and life.

It was a long time before I was able to look forward to something as simple as getting up in the morning. It took a lot longer for my dreams to begin to illuminate my path the way they once had done.

What about *your* dreams? Do you have big-picture plans that you love to ponder in your heart? Or do you feel like you've lost your dreams in the face of the hardships of life?

They say the eyes give windows to the soul.

I say dreams give it wings.

The Power of a Dream

I was one of those precocious little kids who knew exactly what she wanted to be when she grew up — and would tell folks in a heartbeat. People would peer down at me and say, "So, what do you want to be when you grow up, little girl?" And without batting an eye I would say, "A famous writer."

I was spouting poetry practically before I was potty trained. I "published" a neighborhood magazine when I was eleven. I wrote stories in my bed after everyone else was asleep, holding a flashlight underneath my chin. I took Yearbook in high school, and bypassed the college I wanted to attend for a different school that had a bigger journalism major.

I always knew.

Last year I got a call from Ramona Tucker at *Today's Christian Woman* magazine inviting me to be a contributing editor. My ten-minute victory dance around the living room was cut short only because, after awhile, the look of total mortification on the face of my adolescent daughter got kind of distracting.

I grabbed Kaitlyn by the hand and whisked her to the bookcase in the den. "I've got to show you something," I giggled, and caught a glimmer of interest in her face despite the fact that she was trying very hard to appear very cool and very bored.

I pulled out a scrapbook with a smiley face sticker on the front, then flipped dog-eared pages until I found what I was looking for: Between pressed flowers and snapshots of first boyfriends was a brittle newspaper clipping featuring photos of nineteen teenage girls, all vying for the beauty pageant title of "Miss Downey."

There I was, middle left, sporting a Farrah Fawcett 'do (it was 1976, after all). Beneath my photo were these words: "Sixteen-year-old Karen Scalf hopes someday to become either an author or magazine editor."

I showed Kaitlyn the clipping with glee. "See? Right there. There it is. I'm doing it, Kaitlyn. Of course, I'm not actually a magazine editor, but I'm part of the team! Isn't that great? I had a dream, and it's coming true. Your dreams can come true too!"

She rolled her eyes and said, "Oh, Mom." Except the word was pronounced "Maaa-umm," in the way adolescents have of turning your name into a multi-syllabic protest of some kind. Toss in a Texas accent, and we're talking five syllables, maybe six.

But behind the cool exterior, I think she shared my excitement, because that night when she told the whole story to my husband, I noticed that she no longer looked mortified. Mildly embarrassed, yes, but mortified, no. I took it as a good sign.

Top Ten List for Dreamers

Dreams.

How do we know which ones are going to come true?

Does it matter?

Just the fact that we are capable of having big dreams is a wonderful gift. I know, because I've lived without my dreams, and it's no picnic.

Dreams are the footpaths we take to accomplishments and experiences that we probably wouldn't have stumbled across without a trail. If we can envision something in our minds, chances are we can create it in our reality. And even if we can't, just the experience of nurturing a dream — even a dream that turns out to be unattainable — can lift our spirits, expand our boundaries, broaden our thinking, and exercise our imaginations.

What are your dreams? I know, let's make a list. Let's write down ten dreams. Ten things we've always wanted to do in life. Ten goals or aspirations. Some might seem crazy (one of my friends would like to go back and experience life in the seventeenth century), but if you've pondered it in your heart, write it on your list.

I asked some friends of mine to do this very thing.

Nancy's list included going to London and seeing a play, becoming a wildlife photographer, going white-water rafting, learning to water ski, and living in a rustic cabin. She said she also wanted to become a naturalist, which alarmed the rest of us because we've heard you can get arrested for that in some states, not to mention the risk of sun damage to tender parts of the anatomy exposed to daylight for the first time. Nancy said she meant a person who studies plants. (Which means I can relax. It also means I need to remember to take her name off the prayer chain at church.)

Darla's list included owning a resort, going to chef school, crossing the ocean on an old-style cruise liner (preferably one without Leonardo DiCaprio on its guest registry), and learning to play the violin.

My list? Learning to dance the "Achy Breaky Heart," taking a woodworking class, making the bestseller list one day, having my own radio show, renovating an old farmhouse, and creating a whimsical, rambling garden in my backyard.

Your turn. What does your list look like?

Go ahead. Make a list. Ten things.
I'll wait.

Yes, I mean now.

Look, if this'll help, I'll leave some space where you can write your list. Now get going. Use a pencil so you can erase it later if you want. Just get started:

_____

_____

_____

_____

_____

_____

_____

_____

_____

_____

Thank you.

Now. Are there any items on your list that you're working toward right now? I know I'm working on the item from my list regarding my garden — we just put up a swing set, I planted bulbs last week, and

I've got edging waiting for the new flower bed I'm digging. What about you? There might be items on your list that are "works in progress." If so, give yourself a star.

Literally.

Draw a star by your dreams in progress.

Now review your list. My guess is there is another dream hiding there, something attainable, something you could begin to turn into reality.

Two days after I asked her to make her list, Darla announced: "Guess what? I found a violin!"

She had invited us for Sunday lunch, and we were sitting around her dining room table eating Oreos when she broke the news. Her husband blinked. "Violin? What's this about a violin?"

Darla beamed. "Karen knows. It was one of my dreams. And today I talked to someone from church who said I could borrow her violin. Plus, Nancy used to play in a school orchestra, and she's promised to give me lessons!"

Your turn. Draw a circle around an attainable dream. What do you need to do to take the first step? Locate a violin? Make a phone call? Take a class? Read a book? Talk to an expert?

Take a first step today.

No More Excuses!

What keeps us from pursuing our dreams? Sometimes we're so bogged down in daily living, we think we don't have the energy to chase a dream. What we don't realize, however, is that striving to make a dream come true often generates more energy than it takes. Dreams are motivators.

Another reason we may not pursue big dreams is that we're afraid if we reach for a dream we might fall short and experience . . . drum roll, please . . . *failure!* Of course, in my mind this makes about as much sense as saying if we go for a swim we might get wet. Let's settle this once and for all: OF COURSE WE'RE GOING TO FAIL. And it's a good thing, too. Our failures are, indeed, stepping-stones to success. Believe it or not, we learn far more from our failures than from our successes. Sure, success is more fun, but for the lessons we need in order to accomplish our goals, nothing is as beneficial as a sound failure now and then.

Failure is a stepping-stone. It becomes a tragedy only when we refuse to go any farther, setting up housekeeping on the stony path when we could have lived in a mansion if we'd only continued down the trail.

What other reasons do we have for not pursuing our dreams? How about not enough time? I've used this excuse as much as the next woman, but the fact is, it doesn't hold water. My mom once told me that it's amazing what you can accomplish if you set aside thirty minutes a day to pursue your goal. Thirty minutes a day! I spend more time than that reading junk mail and watching TV commercials.

Her words inspired me greatly. She's right! If I invested thirty minutes a day practicing the piano, walking the treadmill, or puttering in my garden, what might I be able to accomplish?

Some goals require a huge chunk of time. A lot of dreams, however, can be achieved by investing little more than left-over minutes from our days.

The Care and Feeding of Big Dreams

If you have big dreams, you have already reaped big benefits, regardless of whether or not your dream materializes into reality. I'll bet you didn't know that Albert Einstein once said: "Imagination is more important than knowledge." Dreaming stretches our imaginations and is a worthwhile endeavor for that reason alone!

And if dreams are good, dreams that come true are even better. For the best chance of seeing some of your dreams come true, consider these suggestions:

Divide and conquer. Remember the movie *What about Bob?* starring Bill Murray? Bill's zany character becomes the overzealous fan of a psychologist who writes a book encouraging "baby steps" toward mental health. Of course, the goal of the movie was to make us laugh, not provide a commentary on achieving our dreams. It accomplishes both.

Dividing a big dream into a series of baby steps can take something that once seemed unattainable and put it very much within our reach. Writing a 200-page book, for example, may seem formidable. Writing a single page, however, is well within reach. Repeat that same baby step five days a week for one year, and your book is done. Think about some of your goals. Can you break a major goal into a series of tiny ones? If so, you're halfway there.

Redefine failure and success. Sandra Glahn writes about a ten-year struggle with infertility in her book *When Empty Arms Become a Heavy Burden* (Broadman and Holman, 1997). Eventually Sandra and her husband conceived and gave birth to daughter Alexandra. But by then, Sandra had learned how to look at "success" and "failure" in a whole new light. She writes: "God defines success not in terms of what we accomplish; He defines it in terms of the transformation we allow His word to make in our lives. I am a success if I can get through my experience with a greater love for God and my spouse than when I started. I am a success on some days if in spite of my lack of 'success' I manage to drag myself out of bed, get dressed, and find reasons to be thankful for one more day."

Don't limit yourself by viewing success and failure as a single, narrow path. Ask God to show you his perspective when it comes to our dreams and goals.

Embrace risk. Yes, yes, I know what I said about baby steps. But every now and then, making a dream come true means taking a gigantic leap. If a rare opportunity presents itself, weigh the cost, then consider going for it.

Notice I said "weigh the cost," not "weigh the odds." Even if the odds are against you, if the cost in dollars, time, or emotional and physical energy is one you are willing to pay, then don't let slim odds deter you. That's why it's called "risk."

Admit who you are. I spent a lot of years telling myself and people around me that I wanted to be a writer someday. Then, somewhere along the way — my guess is that I was in my late teens — I heard a speaker say to his audience, "Stop thinking of yourself as a wanna-be. Begin today telling yourself and others *who you are.*"

From that point, I changed my thinking and my terminology as well. I began telling myself and others, "I am a writer." It seemed silly at first, since my body of published works consisted of articles for my high school paper and the poem I got published in a magazine for Girl Scouts (and for which, I might add, I was paid five dollars — I remember because I framed the check). But before long it became second nature. And since I was suddenly thinking of myself as a *bona fide* writer, it became easier to do the things real writers do, like be consistent in sending queries and honing my skills.

Mingle with cheerleaders. The truth is,

some people bring doom and gloom wherever they go. Their negative attitudes could depress a roomful of monkeys on a caffeine high. I'd wager even Norman Vincent Peale would have a hard time harnessing the power of positive thinking in their presence. When Kaitlyn was younger, she sometimes confused the word "pessimist" with "pesticide." She may have been on to something. After all, we don't call people like that "killjoys" for nothing. These are not the kind of folks we want to share our dreams with, ladies.

When I began writing my book *Pillow Talk*, I made the mistake of showing my first chapter to a friend who apparently did not understand the fragile ecology of a dream. She spent twenty minutes giving unsolicited criticism that virtually tore my efforts to shreds. I'm not particularly thin-skinned about my work, but these comments weren't about my work. They were quite personal in nature. I don't think she was trying to be harsh — but she wasn't being at all careful, and I came away from the encounter with my spirit crushed. It took me six weeks to brush myself off and begin writing again.

To survive and thrive, our dreams need TLC. Of course, there's nothing wrong

Are Your Dreams a Little Out of Tune? Rent a Movie That'll Make Your Heart Sing!

Here are ten movies that will inspire you to greater things! Their message is as powerful as it is simple: *You can do it!*

> *Rudy*
> *Mr. Mom*
> *Baby Boom*
> *Wild Hearts Can't Be Broken*
> *Hook*
> *Iron Will*
> *Places in the Heart*
> *Chariots of Fire*
> *Operation Dumbo Drop*
> *City Slickers*

with constructive criticism, but make a habit of surrounding yourself with folks who are, by nature, encouragers rather than pesticides.

117

Bond with a mentor. Do you know someone who has traveled a little farther down the road you are pursuing? If you do, there's a chance she would enjoy sharing with you her secrets of success. Be sensitive, however: If you sense that she is evasive, or might be feeling threatened by your pending success, then find another mentor.

Look for someone who has experienced the dream you would like to claim for your own, someone who seems to take a genuine interest in your success, someone who talks freely about her own journey and is willing to help you on yours.

Inspire yourself with "can-do" stories. Don't you just love stories where someone beats the odds to make a dream come true? These kinds of *Rocky Balboa* stories are everywhere — the morning newspaper, movies, biographies and autobiographies, and very likely among your own friends.

If you are trying to pursue a dream — or if your dreams have died and you wish you could rekindle the old sparks again — build up your heart and soul by watching and reading "can-do" stories that celebrate the strength and magic inherent in the human spirit.

Give yourself a mental picture to follow.

They say a picture's worth a thousand words. So give yourself a picture of what your dream might look like in real life.

When I was a girl, my family dreamed about one day owning a ranch. My sisters and I created a scrapbook filled with pictures of rugged landscapes and cowboys and livestock, everything we believed represented our dream. Of course, the best pictures were the Marlboro ads, which featured dusty cowboys in rugged settings. The cigarettes hanging out of their mouths were a problem, though. I can't tell you how many hours I spent cutting and pasting in an effort to camouflage those cigarettes!

Start a scrapbook and begin filling it with images that say something to you about your dream. Want to run the Boston Marathon? Look for images of runners and other athletes, as well as articles about people who have achieved impressive athletic feats. Want to create a garden paradise in your backyard? Clip magazine pictures of the kinds of flower landscapes you want to create. Over the years, look for pictures — and words that paint a picture — that can create positive images you can study. You will, quite literally, be providing your mind with a blueprint you can follow as you continue working toward your goal.

Once again, here are the steps:

Divide and conquer.
Redefine failure and success.
Embrace risk.
Admit who you are.
Mingle with cheerleaders.

Bond with a mentor.
Inspire yourself with "can-do" stories.
Give yourself a mental picture to follow.

The unfortunate fact is that, despite our best efforts, our dreams don't always come true. Indeed, we can experience great pain when a beloved dream crashes and burns. And yet, even as we sift through the ashes of one dream, we often find the stirrings of hope for another.

That's the beauty of the human spirit. In fact, the capacity to dream is, I believe, a key indicator of mental and emotional health. After all, a dream is little more than a kind of passionate hope, and without hope, we die. It's as simple as that.

Take stock of your dreams. Measure

their health. If necessary, look back through the years and resurrect some of the dreams from your childhood.

Nurture your dreams, and they will nurture you in return.

Simplify Your Life

Ever feel, well, like you're . . . ahem . . . losing your marbles? You know what I'm talking about. You find yourself doing and saying things that you simply would not do or say if you were playing with a full deck.

Last week we were watching *The Wonder Years* on cable when I turned to my potty training three-year-old and said calmly, "Kacie, if you need to pee-pee, I want you to run real fast and go pee-pee in your bed."

My older daughter stared at me as if I had suddenly sprouted feathers and fur.

I said, "What? What are you staring at?"

"Mom, you just told Kacie to go pee-pee in her bed!"

I blinked. Those words did sound kind

of familiar. Suddenly it all came back to me. I remembered it all. Every horrifying syllable.

Yes, I had indeed said those very words.

It dawned on me that this was not a particularly good sign.

J. M. Barrie Would Be Proud

It's one thing to say things I don't think I'm thinking. Then there is a second category of foibles. These experiences have to do with thinking something that just doesn't add up. Take, for example, the e-mail I received from a friend of mine, Tim Wildmon. Tim is vice president of the American Family Association. The first week in April he dropped me a note by e-mail, in which he mentioned that he was playing the role of Peter in his church drama.

As the mother of a preschooler, I think I probably need to get out of the house more often. I say this because I immediately assumed that the "Peter" Tim would be portraying was none other than *Peter Pan*. In fact, I have to confess that an image of Tim in green tights came rather quickly to mind.

Now the really scary part is that none of

this seemed the least bit odd to me.

Several minutes later I remembered that we were two weeks from Easter. That made me think of church, spiritual things, Easter pageants, Jesus and his disciples.

I hit my palm to my forehead. Oh! THAT Peter.

I felt silly for thinking that Tim's acting debut was as Peter Pan. What was wrong with my thinking? Why had I jumped to such an implausible conclusion? And why didn't I recognize my conclusion as odd even as it was frolicking through my mind? What kind of mental misfire would even cause that kind of thinking?

Besides. Tim doesn't even *own* a pair of green tights.

Okay, I'll admit it. I asked.

A Whole New Meaning for the Phrase "Hard Drive"

Yes, sometimes I say things I'm not thinking. And sometimes I think things that don't make sense. Then, every now and then, I don't think at all. My body is in motion but my brain is not in gear. The lights may be on, but no one's home. The elevator's not going all the way to the top floor. I'm two cards short of a complete deck. One lamb chop short of a full grill.

This is the only way I can begin to explain what happened yesterday morning. In fact, it makes the Pee-Pee Incident and Peter Pan Debacle seem like the work of the Mensa Society.

It all began when Larry and I were preparing to drive to the airport so he could catch a plane for a conference in Indiana. We were loading his bags in the trunk when the phone rang inside the house. I ran inside to catch the call. Moments later, I got behind the wheel of my Honda, and somehow, in the process of pulling out of the driveway, I managed to, . . . um . . . backovermyhusband'sportablecomputerwithmy-car.

Yes, you heard me right. Let me just say that it's probably in my favor that the homicide laws in Texas are so tough. If they weren't, it's hard telling how the story would have ended.

I imagine you want the autopsy report on the computer. Actually, it pulled through. We lost the computer carrier, though — too many lacerations and a broken zipper. The computer itself suffered two broken keys (which Larry was able to repair), a small dent in the casing, and one bent serial port (I can't remember if it was for the Apple Jacks or Shredded Wheat).

And I guess to be entirely accurate, I should make a minor correction. I didn't back completely over the computer. From the skid marks on the driveway it appears that I only caught the computer with one of the rear tires of my Honda and ground it into the concrete for two yards. See? Isn't that a relief?

Sigh. The scary part is that all three incidents took place in the span of less than a week. Which leaves me with one question. I'm kinda' enjoying those old reruns of *The Wonder Years*. Can anyone tell me if they've got cable at the Funny Farm?

Dementia and Stress:

Coincidence or Cohorts?

Maybe you've had similar experiences. You consider yourself a reasonably rational, intelligent, clear-thinking individual. And then you experience a season when your thoughts seem foggy and distracted at best.

Brain tumor? Alzheimer's? Alien interference from outer space?

I guess anything's possible. But chances are, what you're dealing with is a simple, reversible, non-terminal, alien-free, old-fashioned case of teeth-grinding, brain-clogging STRESS!

That's right. When we're stressed by negative influences or emotions in our lives — crisis, depression, anger, disappointment, overcommitment, and more — we can become preoccupied. We can lose the sharp edge that usually characterizes our thinking. We can lose clarity of thought. We can even feel muddled or sluggish in our responses to life. Even making simple decisions can feel overwhelming at times.

Sometimes it feels as though the 101 balls I'm juggling are falling in chaos around me. I can't keep up. I can't keep track. I forget important details. Even simple decisions loom like ominous clouds. I'm losing control of my world, and I'm not sure if the problem is all in my head, or if my head *is* the problem. Is it just my imagination or did I manage to lose some brainpower along the way?

So what's the solution? If our emotional files are too full, our Daytimers are crammed, and our brains are blinking O V E R-

L O A D! in neon letters and threatening to crash the system at any moment, what can we do about it? Who can we call? Where can we go? What is the answer that will save us from ourselves?

I have one word of advice:

Delete.

Less Is More

Want to clear your head? Simplify your life.

Take out the trash, and I'm not just talking about last night's pizza boxes. There are lots of things that create unnecessary clutter in our lives. Want some examples?

Are there piles of laundry, paperwork, and unfinished crafts cluttering our homes? A cluttered environment can render us distracted and overwhelmed. And what about time-wasters cluttering our schedules? Time-wasters can leave us feeling unfocused and unproductive.

Junk food is another culprit: It clutters our systems and can actually impair concentration.

And what about emotional clutter? Are there useless — even destructive — attitudes and emotions that are getting in the way of healthy perspectives? Finally, what about expectations? Do we have unrealistic expectations cluttering our lives and generating unnecessary stress?

We might think, "Simplify my life? But what would I get rid of?!" The truth is, we might be surprised at all the unnecessary baggage creating stress and distraction in our lives.

Simplify Your Life

So how can we begin weeding from our lives the unnecessary and the distracting? When life seems to be spinning out of control, how can we reduce, delete, streamline, and downsize in ways that will make it all seem manageable again?

You know, when I think of the word "manageable" I think of shampoo. After all, isn't that what all those shampoo manufacturers are always promising us? Manageable hair. Do we have split ends, greasy roots, fly-away hair, or flaky follicles? All we have to do is use Wonder Shampoo, and our hair will be manageable again. Bad hair days are what happen when we use *other* companies' hair care products. For

TRULY manageable hair, it's got to be Wonder Shampoo all the way. Wonder Shampoo strips away all the yucky residue left from other hair care products, washes away dandruff, dirt, and oil, and leaves us with a natural looking shine and lots of bounce and body too.

Wouldn't it be great if there was a product that could do the same for the rest of our lives? Strip away the yucky residue, wash out unwanted build-up, and leave us with a new bounce in our steps?

I actually saw a shampoo recently that promised a new, patented anti-fatigue formula. Forget my follicles. They can take care of themselves. Just give me some of that anti-fatigue formula in a tall glass. No ice.

So how can we begin to simplify our lives into something a little more manageable? Let's take a hint from the shampoo companies and look at seven tips designed to help us strip away residue, wash out unwanted build-up, experience less fatigue, and even put new bounce in our steps:

Seize the Day

It's so easy to lament the past or fret about the future. And yet the only thing I'm being asked to manage at the moment is the twenty-four-hour window of time called today. Twenty-four hours, minus the six or seven I spend in sleep. That's maybe seventeen hours. I can do that!

Organizational gurus tell us that even an overwhelming project can be managed easily if we divide it into bite-sized chunks. Our lives can feel overwhelming at times. But luckily for you and for me, God in his great wisdom has already mastered that bite-sized chunk concept. Focus on today. Make the most of today. That makes things simpler right there, doesn't it?

Have a Garage Sale

Whether you have a curbside sale, call the Goodwill truck, or give the trash man a hernia from hefting all your discards, the point is to declutter your home. Simplify your environment. It's amazing how a clutter-free environment can reduce stress and clarify thinking.

When I was struggling with clinical

depression, I wondered if going to work outside of my home might be a solution. Taking a job, I reasoned, would get me out of the house and in the midst of other people. I wouldn't feel so isolated. About that time, I learned of an editorial position at a major Christian publishing company thirty minutes from my home. I interviewed for the job just before Christmas. The publisher's last words to me were, "Let's get together after the holidays and talk salary."

Confident the job was mine, I realized I was about to make a major transition. I figured I had a month, at best, to get my house in tip-top shape before starting my new job. I cleaned closets and organized drawers. I blasted through piles of clutter. I kept the trash collector and the Goodwill truck busy for weeks.

Soon my house was spotless. I was living clutter-free. And you know what? Suddenly my depression didn't seem so overwhelming anymore. I could think more clearly than I had been able to think in a long time. And now that my house was clutter-free, I felt freer to have lunch with girlfriends or take my daughter to the park. My isolation began to lift as well.

Did cleaning my house cure my depression? Hardly. But I discovered a distinct link between a cluttered environment and cluttered, unfocused thinking.

What happened to my new job? I have no idea. We never spoke again. For some reason known only to them, they never called back. My dad kept urging me to call the company and find out whether I had the position. Each time he did, I heard myself saying, "I will, but not yet. I'm not ready yet. I still want to have lunch with so-and-so and finish sewing the bedroom curtains and write another magazine article."

Basically, I was having too much fun to get a real job. Looking back, I see now that taking that position would have been a huge mistake. I didn't need to add a fifty-hour-a-week career position onto my already full platter of freelance writing and parenting responsibilities. But thinking about the position motivated me to declutter my life, and that in turn reduced my stress and gave me new focus and freedom.

For me, winning the war against depression meant fighting a great number of lesser battles. Decluttering my environment was one of many small victories that, in the end, helped me to win the war.

Want to simplify your life? Then simplify your expectations. Life is filled with foibles, flaws, and imperfections. Expecting life to be perfect . . . or our performance to be perfect . . . or our children, spouses, parents, or friends to be perfect . . . well, there's no quicker ticket to the Funny Farm.

I had just finished delivering a speech at a women's luncheon when a young mother approached me with a dilemma. Wringing her hands, she said, "I don't know what to do with my two-year-old. He challenges everything I say! I'm at my wit's end and don't know how to handle him."

I held her hands. "For starters, don't take his behavior personally. This is not about you."

"It's not?"

"He's two, right? Then he's just doing his job. In fact, it sounds like he's being very conscientious about it! A two-year-old is SUPPOSED to challenge every boundary known to humankind. It's in his job description. Look. Don't expect him to act like an adult, then take it personally when he doesn't. Instead, anticipate disobedience and then be calm and ready with whatever consequence you promised he would receive for his infraction. Be consistent with your discipline. And when his behavior requires discipline, don't view it as a failure, either his or yours. Instead, see it for what it is — a teaching opportunity. In fact — dare I say it? — look forward to those times when you can, lovingly and calmly, enforce a promised ramification. The lessons he's learning today, at two, will go a long way toward helping him make better choices when he is ten, twenty, and beyond."

Was there anything unusual about the behavior of this toddler? Not really. But his mother's expectations were paving the way for added stress and frustration.

You and I are guilty of the same thing, aren't we? We want well-behaved lives, lives that don't talk back, slough off, or mess up. We want our lives to emulate Emily Post. No wonder we're upset when our lives are more accurately characterized by Lucy Ricardo.

We want our years on this earth to be a piece of cake, a bed of roses, a walk in the park. What we forget is that cakes have calories and roses have thorns. And as for a walk in the park, the last time I took a walk in the park I stepped in dog poop.

If we want to simplify our lives, abandoning unrealistic, pie-in-the-sky expectations is a good place to start. In marriage, parenting, and self-care, we've got to learn to laugh and roll with the punches, cherishing life despite its imperfections.

Minister to Others

You know, kids think the world revolves around them, don't they? Take Kacie, for example. One day she was playing blocks in the den while I was sitting on the couch, remote in hand, surfing through the TV channels. At one point I stopped roving long enough to observe a TV preacher. He was good, although a little brimstonesque. His speech was bold-faced, underlined, and punctuated by exclamation points. If he had been preaching in front of a punching bag, it would have been swaying.

About that time, Kacie looked up from her toys and asked fretfully, "Mama, why is that man yelling at me?"

I had to laugh. "He's not yelling at you, Kacie. He's on the TV. He can't even see you."

She looked relieved. "Oh."

Sometimes I wonder if I'm not just like

Kacie. Do I have a skewed perspective on my world? Does it all revolve around me, me, me? Is my life overly wrapped up in my own issues, needs, and perspectives?

You know, you can get away with that when you're three. At thirty-eight, it becomes a little harder to justify.

Want to simplify your life? Take your eyes off yourself and focus on ministering to someone else.

About a year ago I got heavily involved in the life of a young mother who was about to walk out on her husband. I spent hours counseling and praying with her. We searched Scriptures together. We cried together.

Each evening when my little family was reunited, I looked at the faces around me and I knew that I was blessed. Somehow, in the light of the pain in the life of my friend, my own world didn't seem so complicated anymore. The fight Larry and I had last week . . . well, I realized now how very trivial it was. The challenges of parenting and making a living . . . they were miniscule when compared to the challenges my friend was facing as she agonized over a marriage gone bad.

When we reach out to people around us, we not only make an impact on other lives, but sometimes we get a clearer perspective on our own. Maybe we're encouraging a friend one-on-one, or volunteering to help a local charity, or taking a meal to someone in need. The point is to get our focus off ourselves and meet a need for someone else. We'll find that our own lives make more sense as a result.

Prioritize on Paper

My dad does a lot of speaking on leadership issues. (In fact, contact Gene at genescalf@net999.com if your church or company is looking for a truly dynamic speaker.) Anyway, a story he often tells has to do with this very thing, this idea that you can master at least a part of your life with a yellow legal pad and a Bic. The following true story always had an impact on me, and it just might mean something to you as well.

Many years ago Charles Schwab, president of United States Steel Corporation and Ivy Lee, one of the leading business consultants in New York, were having lunch together when Schwab remarked that he wished he could get more organized productivity from his employees.

After a brief discussion, Ivy Lee made the statement that he had the solution and he wrote the answer on a piece of paper and gave it to Schwab.

As Schwab looked at it, he commented that it looked simple enough and asked Ivy how much he owed him. Ivy Lee told him to try it and pay him what it was worth. Several months later Ivy Lee received a check from United States Steel Corporation for $25,000 (several *hundred* thousand dollars in today's economy!).

What was the hastily jotted down idea that was so valuable to Mr. Schwab? Simply this: Every day have your employees make a list of things they want to accomplish that day and number them according to importance. Then work on No. 1 until it is finished. Then go on to No. 2, and then No. 3, and so on . . . until the list is finished or the day is over. The next day do the same thing.

If I might be allowed to summarize the thought:

Making a list
And checking it twice
Can transform your schedule
From naughty to nice!

About a year ago I went through a tough time. In fact, I sat down with Larry in the den one night and laid my cards on the table.

"Larry, I'm slipping," I said frankly. "I'm losing it and I'm afraid I'm going to slip back into the depression."

The fact is, I was succumbing to stress. I was overcommitted and overexposed and overwhelmed as a result.

Then and there, Larry got a pad and pen and we began to brainstorm. How could we simplify? What steps could we take to make life feel "manageable" again? We came up with five action points and began putting them into practice the next day.

Several of them focused on obtaining help for "problem areas" in our lives. Housework is always a huge stresser for me. Keeping our three-quarters-acre yard trimmed and mowed is consuming too. Finally, Larry and I own a small four-plex in California, and trying to keep the place rented and maintained from Texas had long been a source of tremendous pressure.

We knew we needed help.

We immediately set about renting out a spare room in our home and used the money to hire a high schooler to mow our lawn, as well as a cleaning service to help with housework once a week. Then we found a property management company in California and turned over the keys (and the headaches) of our four-plex.

Like I said, that was a year ago. We still use the property management company. David still mows occasionally, though not often. And I went from hiring a cleaning service weekly to twice a month, and now only when the piles get so high I have to walk next door to find a phone, meaning every two or three months.

See? Admitting you need help doesn't mean you're locked into a long-term commitment. You can always make adjustments based on how you're feeling. And if cash flow is a problem, trade "services" with friends. Say, "I'm really feeling overwhelmed right now. If you'd be game to come over and help me clean house for a couple hours, I'll come over next week and help you wallpaper that bathroom you've been meaning to finish."

Observe Moral Principles

There's another way to simplify our lives, and it can be summed up in four little words: "Do the right thing." Remember the saying, "What a tangled web we weave when first we practice to deceive"? Talk about stress and complexities! When we don't live our lives according to any moral standard . . . when we make all of our decisions based on a sliding scale . . . when we give ourselves permission to lie or twist the truth . . . our lives can get really complicated, really fast.

On the other hand, when we live by a healthy moral code, things get so much simpler. Should I tell the cashier that the one cookie sheet she rang up is actually *two* sheets stuck together? If I live by a moral code, there's no stress here. I know exactly what to do.

Should I fudge on my income tax? If I live by a code, the answer's simple.

Should I fantasize about someone who is off-limits to me? Have an affair? Lie to my husband about the credit card bill? Pass along a bit of juicy news even though it was shared with me in confidence?

These are no-brainers . . . as long as I have a code to guide me.

You want to see how complicated life can become when moral standards are compromised? Just turn on the TV and watch Jerry Springer or Jenny Jones do their stuff. (On

Want to simplify your life? Get in the habit of asking yourself these questions whenever you're feeling stressed:

Will this matter ten years from now?

Where will I store this?

Why am I doing this?

Can I live without this?

What will I remove from my schedule or my home in order to make room for this?

Is this causing more trouble and stress than it's worth?

Is there an easier way of doing this?

Does this need to be done perfectly . . . or just get done?

Is this the best choice for me right now?

second thought, just take my word for it. Never let it be said that I recommended *The Jerry Springer Show* to a living soul.)

Trust me when I say that the studio stages are filled with men and women reaping whirlwinds of complexity usually because, somewhere along the way, they got out of the habit of doing the right thing. The themes of the show are a dead giveaway, with titles like "We Once Had a One Night Stand but Now I'm Married to Your Poodle's Shrink," or "My Lover Paid for My Implants, but His Check Was Hot and Now They Want These Babies Back."

If you and I live by a moral code, does that mean our lives will never feel stressed or complex?

Of course not. But when we make the healthiest choices we can make — each and every day — no matter what trauma and stress comes into our lives at least we'll have the comfort of knowing that we did our best. Maybe we'll sleep better at night. Besides, as stressful as life gets, the chances are good that we're going to avoid the *added* stress that comes with a lifetime of making REALLY bonehead decisions.

They say you reap what you sow.

Sow wise choices.

Reap peace.

Clean Up Your Act

Want to wash that stress right out of your hair?

Seize the day.

Have a garage sale.

Abandon unrealistic expectations.

Minister to others.

Prioritize on paper.

Obtain help when necessary.

Observe moral principles.

You and I will never obtain stress-free living. And that's okay. Without *some* stress, life would be pretty boring. The good news is that — with a little effort — you can strip away residue, wash out unwanted build-up, experience less fatigue, and even put new bounce in your step.

Best yet, you'll never have to explain to your husband why there are tire treads on his mouse.

No Trespassing

I've been wanting to write a chapter on *privacy* but I'm having a hard time remembering the precise definition of the word. All I can remember is that it has something to do with a commodity I used to have, and now I don't.

I can't look up the word in my dictionary because my dictionary's been missing ever since my daughter borrowed it for a homework assignment.

I can't use my very own personal computer to look it up on the Internet because my husband, wanting to try out some new software, loaded a program onto my computer, and now it keeps malfunctioning and hinders me from using my modem.

I meant to ask my friend Cherie for the

definition of the word *privacy* when she was over yesterday. Unfortunately, I kept getting distracted by my three-year-old repeatedly climbing onto my lap and poking her fingers in my nose.

I'll be the first to admit that my husband and children are treasures that enrich my life to no end. I wouldn't trade them for anything the world has to offer. Do I want gold? Brushing and braiding Kacie's flaxen hair provides plenty of that. Elegant music? Kaitlyn's laughter will suffice. Fine wine? I'll take the kisses of my man any day. The finer things of life are already in my home.

But contrary to popular belief, the best things in life are hardly free. All this rich living comes with a price. And one of the costs, quite frankly is . . .

. . . what's that word again?

Oh yeah.

Privacy.

Private: No Trespassing

It's nice to be sought after. But sometimes you can get too much of a good thing. My pet peeve is hearing a knock on the bathroom door followed by the familiar words, "What are you doing in there?"

What do they think I'm doing?

Maybe kids have this weird fear that, while their bathroom time is reserved for boring functions of elimination, grown-ups aren't bound by the same rules. Maybe they think we hide out in the bathroom so we can do really cool things we don't let *them* do, like eating Gummi Bears before dinner and watching cartoons when our homework isn't done. That's why we lock the door. We don't want our children to know we're having all the fun.

Not only is bathroom time not sacred but personal space is up for grabs as well. Literally.

I knew a woman who once dressed her seven-year-old daughter as a "Mommy" for Halloween. She put curlers in her daughter's hair, smeared jelly on her shirt, and tied an apron around her waist. But the *pièce de résistance* was the baby doll strapped to her leg.

We all know what that feels like, don't we?

I don't know about your experience with little ones, but my babies didn't believe in pacifiers and security blankets. After all, why should they cling to a threadbare piece of cloth when they could cling to me?

Kaitlyn's comfort item of choice was my earlobe. She hung on when she was bored, scared, or tired. She considered my earrings a very personal affront.

Kacie got a little more personal than that. She's three and she still thinks my right armpit belongs to her. That and my mole. It's on my left shoulder blade. One day she skinned her knee on the driveway. After I patched her up she was still crying. I offered hugs, popsicles, gum, and more. She wouldn't stop crying. Finally, through her tears, she said, "I want your mole." She wrapped her arms around my neck, slipped a hand under my shirt, found my mole, hiccuped once, and stopped crying.

I teach my kids the concept of personal space, and the idea that there are parts of their body that are private. For my daughters, I've described these areas as the parts of the body that would be covered up by a two-piece bathing suit. What I don't tell them is that this definition will apply until they become mothers. Somehow, in the process of conceiving a baby, birthing a baby, and nursing a baby, everything's up for grabs. Between husbands, nurses, doctors, and our newborns, every "private part" we ever had seems to become public property.

I remember when I was giving birth to Kaitlyn. I had just passed my pain threshold and asked — no, begged — for some drugs. In no time at all the Demerol took effect and ushered me into la-la-land. I know I was in la-la-land because I remember looking at my husband and saying thickly, "Honey, could you close the kitchen door? I think I feel a breeze."

Was I in the kitchen? Of course not. That was the Demerol talking. Did I feel a breeze? What do you think? The way the LDR door kept revolving with hospital staff, gusts in that room must have been approaching 20 mph — and me wearing nothing but a paper gown and metal stirrups. No doubt windchill was a major factor. It's a miracle I didn't have to be treated for frostbite at some point after crowning and before my episiotomy. Breeze? That's an understatement: I was experiencing high winds in an area of my anatomy where the sun never shines.

Privacy. Hah!

By the time we're mothers, we don't have any private parts left. The skimpiest bathing suit wouldn't reveal anything we haven't already revealed to total strangers in lab coats.

And what about privacy when it comes

to our personal belongings? We spend years trying to teach our children the nuances of sharing. We talk about greed versus generosity, selfishness versus selfless giving. We model and lecture and teach and inspire. And after we have expended all our words on the subject, what our children manage to conclude from our vast outpouring of wisdom and insights is that what's ours is theirs and what's theirs is theirs, too.

The family car? Theirs. The balance in the checkbook? Theirs. Mom's favorite cashmere sweater and Dad's secret stash of Wintergreen Lifesavers? Theirs, theirs, theirs.

My children have already informed me which pieces of my jewelry they want when I die.

I remember once, when Kaitlyn was about four, feeling tired after a long day filled with Barbies and Big Bird. I felt like I needed a break from my role as Social Director and Principle Plaything for our daughter. She was begging me to play hide-and-seek when I spoke up in frustration: "Kaitlyn, we've been playing for hours! What do you think I am, a toy?"

Kaitlyn looked at me, and without batting an eyelash, said, "Yes."

Well. That explains a lot, doesn't it?

After all, toys are on call twenty-four hours a day. They have no personal space and get no respect. They don't have any possessions. Half the time they don't even get to wear clothes.

But maybe I should count my blessings. I might not get any more privacy than Barbie, but at least my elbows bend.

Benefits of Privacy

Yep, if you're busy raising a family, privacy may be hard to come by. And, yet, there's no denying the rejuvenating power of solitude. When your emotions are feeling bruised for any reason — stress from daily living, tension in relationships, overcommitment, financial pressure, pent up anger, or even just because it's "that time of the month" — a quiet separation from the hubbub of daily life may help you heal, renew, and regroup.

Sometimes privacy can even help us remember who we are. Several years ago I got a phone call from my wonderful mom. She greeted me, then said, "How are you?"

When I said, "Fine!" without any thought, she posed the question again.

"I was not talking about Karen-the-wife, or Karen-the-mother, or Karen-the-writer . . . I want to know about you. How are *you?*"

I laughed a little too quickly. "After all that, Mama, I don't know if there's anyone left."

She laughed with me, but we both knew it wasn't a joke.

Grown-up life is filled with a plethora of projects and responsibilities. There are things to do and places to go and people to love. This is a wonderful thing. This is a privilege. And yet, sometimes in the hustle and bustle it can feel like we're losing ourselves, our sense of control, even our sanity.

Do we want to rediscover these things? Seeking out a little privacy is a great way to begin.

Private Moments

Sometimes we just need some space, don't we? Space to think and sort, maybe stew and fume, and definitely regroup, renew, relax, and, in short, pull ourselves together.

A bubble bath can do wonders. Sneak

your teen's boom box into the bathroom along with a soothing compact disc, light some candles for atmosphere, remove the plastic alligators and toy boats left over from your preschooler's last bath, dump in some fragrant bath crystals (Mr. Bubble will do in a pinch), and then soak away.

Or go for a walk. Preferably at sunset. If your kids want to come, let them ride bikes nearby as you walk. They'll be having so much fun, you'll be practically alone. Close your eyes. Smell the air. Now look at the clouds, a bouquet of red and pink and purple, a parting gift from a chivalrous sun.

Where else can we enjoy a private moment? How about in the midst of our boisterous families? I read about one mom who has learned how to let her family know when she needs to be left alone. She has a favorite, weathered cotton robe. The hem is frayed and the elbows worn, but the robe has "comfort" written all over it. Whenever she feels grumpy or stressed, she slips into her robe and her husband and kids know to give her a wide berth. A few hours later, she's usually ready to rejoin family life with a smile.

What a civil alternative to biting the head off the first family member who says the wrong thing at the wrong time (which is what I tend to do when I'm feeling stressed and on the verge of a mild break-down)!

Sometimes, getting the privacy we need isn't as tough as we make it seem. Sometimes, a little communication goes a long way.

Private Pleasures

Privacy doesn't have to be about giving yourself space away from your family. Sometimes it's about creating space in your busy schedule for pleasures that seem to "speak" to the inner core of who you are.

Puttering around my garden around four o'clock on a spring afternoon does that for me. It doesn't matter if I'm alone, or if Kaitlyn is on the swing set, or Kacie is watering her shoes with the garden hose. The shadows are beginning to lengthen, the day has cooled, and it's always fun to see what horticultural developments have taken place since I was there last. I also love to gaze and let my imagination frolic: What if next year we built a playhouse there? Or put a fountain there? Or planted a peach tree next to that fence?

Going to dinner and a movie with my husband is a private pleasure. It makes me feel like we're dating again. I also enjoy the temporary escape into other worlds characterized by action heroes, lighthearted lovers, or dangerous mysteries (the popcorn's a draw as well. Extra butter, please).

Reading a can't-stop novel until 3:00 A.M. is a private luxury. I know that I'll pay with droopy eyes and cotton thoughts the following day, but I usually think it's worth the price.

Is there space in your day for the pleasures that are special to you?

Private Jokes

We all love private jokes, don't we? To this day my sisters and I will crack up over the phrases "Hi Bob," "Burn, cookie, burn," or "The Scooby-Doo-Cartoon-Dash-out-of-the-Texas-Hailstorm." Sometimes funny things happen when we're with our closest friends that defy explanation. When we try to explain the humor to people who weren't there when it happened, they give us blank stares and we end up shrugging and saying, "I guess you just had to have been there."

In order to stockpile a stash of private jokes, it means spending time getting crazy with people who are special to us. Last weekend, Larry attended a conference in Indianapolis, and Kaitlyn went along so she could visit her grandparents in Anderson, half an hour away. With an empty weekend looming in front of me, I did the only thing that made any sense at the time.

I planned a slumber party.

Cherie couldn't make it, but Beth, Darla, and Nancy all showed up on my doorstep Friday evening with toothbrushes in hand. We watched movies, ate nachos, and stayed up talking 'til three. When friend Tim Wildmon heard about our escapades, he said, "Remember whatever it was you were laughing about at 2:30 in the morning. Those are the conversations to record and remember forever."

He's right. Those silly, goofball moments with friends and family give us something to cherish. Even better, they give us private jokes and reasons to laugh out loud when we're with those loved ones again — and sometimes even when we're not.

Private Places

Do you have a soothing place that feels like it is yours and yours alone? Perhaps it's a chair in your bedroom, or a favorite corner of the couch, or the wooden swing on the back porch. Maybe it's the front seat of your car; perhaps getting behind the wheel and going for a drive leaves you feeling renewed and refreshed.

Gwen Shamblin, founder of the Weigh Down Workshop, talks about a private place that means a lot to her. It's a corner of the living room couch in the middle of the night. She says this is the place she loves to meet with God while everyone else in her home is fast asleep. In fact, she makes an effort to prepare her private place ahead of time with items that will add to her comfort when she's there. She keeps her Bible under the couch where it will be within reach; she makes sure a warm throw is at hand in case the night is chilly; and there's a coaster on the end table, waiting for the cup of hot tea Gwen always brings when she has her rendezvous with God.

Find a niche. Prepare it with the things

you love: favorite magazines, a secret stash of Orange Milano cookies, a cotton throw, your Bible or devotional material, some fresh flowers, even a journal. You know, we spend a lot of hours creating a warm and inviting nest in which to raise our families. Those same skills can be used to create a mini-nest, so to speak, for ourselves. Are we being selfish? I don't think so. When we have a private place to rest, we're better prepared to meet the needs of those who depend on us.

And while we're in our nest, maybe we should take a cue from Gwen. Do you want a private, intimate activity that will leave you refreshed and renewed like nothing else on earth?

Spend time with Jesus. Read about him in the Bible. Read his very own words in the New Testament. Sing songs for him. Then just be quiet for a while.

One day we'll have all the privacy we need. Our children will have flown the coop; the nest will be empty. We won't need to create private niches for ourselves . . . we'll have the whole house.

Those will be good years.

And maybe, if we're very, very blessed, those years will be just as wonderful as the years we spent raising our families.

Being needed is a great thing. And if we're in the midst of raising families and we happen to be needed twenty-four hours a day . . . well, it's still great.

But to keep it that way, we need to renew ourselves with a little privacy now and then. Our hours apart can leave us refreshed and energized. They can remind us who we are. And they can give us an opportunity to focus and plan.

On top of all that, they just might leave us with a deeper appreciation for our families.

Even if they do get us mixed up with Barbie now and then.

The Care and Feeding of a Grudge

Recently a friend of mine made an interesting observation. Alex Douglas said that, in his opinion, women tend to hang on to grudges longer than men do. He wondered if the fact that women are nurturers by nature had anything to do with this. After all, he pointed out, women are maternal creatures wired to nurture and protect. Could it be that we are prone to nurture and protect our grudges?

I thought this was a ridiculous hypothesis and I let Alex know right away that he was on the wrong track. I told him that I, for one, do not nurture my grudges.

Sure, I think about them often, but that doesn't mean I nurture them.

I feed them and chart their growth, *but*

that doesn't mean I nurture them!

OKAY, so I happen to give them NAMES and celebrate their BIRTH-DAYS. I still say THAT DOESN'T MEAN I NURTURE MY GRUDGES!

Okay, maybe I do.

You got a problem with that?

Look. I know they make nasty pets. Really, I do. I know they don't clean up after themselves and they require a lot of care and they've been known to bite the hand that feeds them.

On top of all that, they grow too fast. They can quickly become too big to keep comfortably in the average-sized home. When people look at each other and say, "This house isn't big enough for the both of us," what they really mean is "the three of us." The third party that no one ever talks about is the grudge. Somebody's been overfeeding the family pet. Remember when Alice, newly arrived in Wonderland, ate the cookie in the Rabbit's house and grew until her head lifted the roof? Same thing. And when that happens, something's got to give. Someone's got to go.

It's usually not the grudge.

For some reason, it often seems easier to get rid of a person than a grudge. Maybe it's because grudges are a little like cats. I remember one stray cat we tried to get rid of. For some reason, my dad hated this cat. He put it in the car, drove to a golf course thirteen miles away, set the cat free, and drove away. Three days later it was mewling and yowling at the back door again.

Grudges are like that. They have this really keen sense of direction. They always seem to land on their feet. And they have nine lives. Maybe even more.

Of course, the thing I really hate is when grudges breed. You let a grudge mature, and you're in trouble. You turn around one day and find yourself tripping over a litter of babies. The little critters nip at your heels and surprise you by showing up in places where you'd least expect to find them. I've thought about having my grudges spayed and neutered to keep this kind of thing from happening, but I can't find a vet who seems to know what I'm talking about when I call and inquire about the procedure.

Grudges really aren't very compatible with family life, either. They're very territorial and hostile to anyone who encroaches on their space. We had a toy poodle once. Micky belonged to my mom, and my mom alone. If she was watching TV at night, Micky would curl up next to her and protect her with all the fight of a 200-pound Doberman. No one could get close to my mom without Micky growling and nipping at the intruder.

Grudges do that. When my grudges are really active, no one can get too close to me. Grudges are jealous critters. And they have sharp teeth. Almost as sharp as their tongues.

Sometimes I get tired of the care and feeding of my grudge. I wonder, "What if I got rid of it for good? Sent it far, far away? What if I even (gulp) considered having it put to sleep?"

But then I get all these mixed emotions. For one thing, I feel sort of *guilty*. After all, my grudge has been my constant companion for a lot of years. It's been loyal. Jealous. Faithful. Can I really consider getting rid of it after all we've been through together?

I also begin to feel . . . well, *lonely*. My grudge is a lot of work, but it gives me something in return too. A sense of protection. A sense of self-righteousness. It keeps me company when I'm feeling estranged from the people around me. I get a lot of comfort from my grudge. Am I really ready to give all that up?

Finally, when I think about life without my grudge, I feel *scared*. Life without my pet would be so different. What would it be like? Would I like my new life? Getting rid of my grudge would leave a void. I'd have to rekindle relationships with the people my grudge has kept at bay. Am I ready for that?

Sigh. I used to think of myself as the owner and my grudge as the pet. But sometimes I'm not so sure.

Sometimes I think I'm the one on the leash.

Grudge-Free Living

Why have I included a chapter on grudges in a book about feeling better? It's simple. Grudges deplete our energy, they make us feel isolated and alone, and they keep old wounds from healing. They increase tension and stress in our lives. They compromise our joy and disrupt our sleep. They harden our hearts if not our arteries.

If you're feeling like you need a positive change in your life, consider getting rid of a grudge.

Oh, I make it sound so easy, don't I?

The truth is, grudges arrive packing a BIG suitcase. They usually plan to hang around for a very long time. Compared to most grudges, a Maytag washer will seem temporal, even fickle. You'll go through two, maybe three of these sturdy appliances before a well fed grudge will get up and go on its own accord.

And yet, grudge-free living is worth the effort. Trust me when I say you'll find new energy and joy. You'll experience new intimacy with family members, friends, God, and even with yourself.

So, how do we begin?

The Many Faces of a Grudge

There are many species of grudges. These include anger, bitterness, resentment, disappointment, hatred, jealousy, and even apathy. And they're sly critters too. A wily grudge can move in and set up housekeeping before we're fully aware that it's even there.

I remember the day my sister Michelle took me aside and said, "Karen, you seem so angry. Why are you so angry all the time?"

Her words seemed strange to me. But as

I pondered her comment, it dawned on me that I was angry far more often than I had ever realized. In fact, I was angry almost every morning when I woke up. And now that she mentioned it, I was angry almost every night when I went to bed. Yikes! All of a sudden I saw that I was angry most of the middle hours as well!

What was almost scarier than my anger was the fact that I had been so blinded to its pervasive presence.

Recognizing our grudges is a first step. It's probably not necessary to celebrate their birthdays or add them to our health insurance, but naming them might not actually be a bad idea.

What is the name of your grudge? Anger? Bitterness? Disappointment? And who is the primary target when your grudge bares its teeth? Your husband? A parent? A sibling, child, or friend? Even God?

Recognizing and naming our grudges might not get them out of our lives. But it's a good start. For one thing, now we'll have something to call them when we tell them to leave.

Benefits and Pitfalls of Maintaining Your Grudge

Now that we've given our pets a name, let's take a realistic look at how they impact our lives. How do our grudges lessen the quality of our lives? Circle the symptoms that apply to you when your grudge is active:

physical fatigue

emotional fatigue

headaches

nausea

heartburn

feelings of isolation

tension in relationships

short temper

feeling out of control

a desire to take revenge

coldness or apathy

being unable to control your words and saying things you later regret

loss of sleep

a feeling of deep sadness

Not a pretty picture, is it?

To successfully evict our grudges, it's also important to fully understand what benefits we're enjoying by their presence. We might say with our lips that we want to get rid of our grudges, but if they are giving us protection or comfort in some fashion, our hearts may not be willing to let go of the leash.

What benefits are we deriving from our grudges? Circle any that apply to you:

A vacation from having to do the hard work of relationship. If I'm holding a grudge, I may feel I have an excuse not to fully participate in relationship with the person with whom I'm upset. I may emotionally withdraw a little. I may feel justified in not doing my part to keep the relationship healthy. That means I can fudge on the hard stuff like being vulnerable, communicating openly, or saying I'm sorry when I make a mistake.

Comfort. A grudge is a standing invitation to indulge myself with a pity party whenever I want one.

Permission to engage in behavior that is childish, rude, indulgent, or even self-destructive. After all, it's easier to give myself permission to act inappropriately when I remind myself that this is a reasonable response after what so-and-so did.

Power. Sometimes, holding a grudge can award me with a feeling of power over the poor, hapless person who had the misfortune of crossing me.

Self-righteousness. A grudge is a daily reminder that I'm a far better person than the dolt of dubious character who caused me such pain.

Now look at your benefits. Certain benefits — like comfort — can, at times, be legitimate. But aren't there better sources of comfort than a grudge? Perhaps talking to a wise friend, or reading something that is inspirational, or even making an appointment with a counselor would be healthier choices than nursing a grudge. Besides, is your ultimate goal comfort or healing? Sometimes finding a healthy way to "get over it" is the most comforting choice we can make.

Other benefits, when you really take a closer look, aren't too flattering. In fact, they may very well reveal character flaws that need some attention. If, by looking at the benefits I'm getting from my grudges, I learn that I'm being lazy in a relationship, or I'm making excuses for my bad behavior, or I'm enjoying feeling self-righteous, maybe it's time to take my eyes off the sins of others and take a long look at my own heart.

Forgiveness: A Present I Give to Myself

Grudges usually have a legitimate beginning. Someone does something that causes us pain, and we feel hurt. In truth, we have a right to feel hurt. This is a normal response.

Some offenses are very serious. If we were molested as children, rejected by people who were supposed to love us, or betrayed by close friends, we have every right to feel pain and even anger at the events that transpired.

But here's where the logic can go awry. Too often, we take the matter a step further and conclude: "If I have a right to feel hurt, then I must have a right to feel hurt for a very, very, very long time."

This is where we get into trouble.

Feeling hurt for a very, very, very long time does a lot of damage. Does it damage the person who hurt us? Not nearly as much as it damages you and me. Of course, it's not easy to forgive and forget. Sometimes the process can take months, even years. But we do ourselves a favor when we do everything in our power to walk through the process as quickly and effectively as we can, rather than prolonging the process by protecting and feeding our pain.

One woman told me, "But I can't forgive. If I forgive, I'm condoning the action that hurt me. I'm handing over a *not-guilty* verdict on a platter. I'm giving peace of mind to the person who hurt me. I'm giving him permission to hurt me again."

These lies are the links in the chain that leash us tightly to our grudges.

Let's look at them one by one:

If I forgive, I'm condoning the action that hurt me. I'm handing over a not-guilty verdict on a platter.

Forgiveness doesn't mean that the action was right. It doesn't diminish guilt. Forgiven or not, the person who hurt you is still responsible for his choice, and still accountable to God.

When God forgives us for something we've done, he has the power to not only forgive, but to administer grace. He, and he alone, can render a verdict of not guilty. He can do this because — if our hearts are humble and repentant — he can take our crimes and transfer them, so to speak, to his Son, Jesus, who already took the punishment for these offenses some 2,000 years ago. How could Jesus take the punishment for offenses that you and I hadn't even committed yet? Think of it as some sort of cosmic time warp, an anachronism of the first degree, like watching a movie written to take place during the Civil War and glimpsing a 747 emerge from the clouds over the Battle at Antietam. Imagine! The mistakes and mean-spirited actions you and I committed in the 1990s were present on the shoulders of a Christ crucified nearly 2,000 years ago. We may not understand the details of how it happened, but it's comforting to know that it did.

The point is, God's forgiveness is a mind-boggling, time-bending, hell-whipping concoction of forgiveness, justice, grace, and a "not-guilty" verdict all rolled into one. But that's because he's God. And you, of course, are not.

You don't have the power to absolve people of their guilt, or spare them from justice, or release them from accountability. You can't reassign fault. You can't turn back the hands of time as if the hurt had never happened.

Don't add things to the act of forgiveness that you can't provide. No wonder you're hesitant to forgive if you believe your forgiveness does all those things. Your decision to forgive is powerful. But it isn't *that* powerful. For that kind of forgiveness, the person who hurt you needs to appeal to a Higher Court.

I'm giving peace of mind to the person who hurt me.

Sure, it's possible that the person who hurt you will sleep better at night knowing she's forgiven. But forgiveness isn't really about giving a gift to the person who hurt you. Forgiveness is a gift that you give yourself.

When you forgive, you are freeing yourself of the exhausting and debilitating responsibility of being the self-appointed keeper-of-the-memory-of-the-pain. What a gift! Not even a box of chocolates comes close!

When you forgive, do you know whose sleep will improve? Yours. Do you know whose peace of mind will multiply? Yours. When you forgive, you take back control of your life. If someone hurt you ten years ago, the hurt might have been great enough to rob you of joy and peace of mind for a week, or a month, or maybe even several years while you healed. But why give away any more hours of your life than absolutely necessary? Cut your losses and take back what is rightfully yours: joy, peace of mind, sound sleep, emotional health, freedom from anger.

Forgiveness is a gift. Give it freely and the real goodies belong to you.

I'm giving him permission to hurt me again.

Healthy boundaries — not grudges — are the best defense against future hurts. If you want to protect yourself, let go of the grudge and learn to embrace good boundaries instead. Learn how to say no to undeserved blame, unwarranted criticism, misplaced anger, and inappropriate comments. Learn how to grow your own sense of self-worth, so you're not dependent on handouts from others. Practice commitment to your values and convictions, and don't give anyone permission to talk you into thoughts or actions that are out of sync with your heartfelt beliefs. Make moral choices to avoid many of the complications, chaos, and catastrophic ramifications of immoral living.

These are the skills that can help protect you from future hurt.

As far as your guardian grudge — well, when it comes to things that go bump in the night, he's all bark and no bite. And even at that, he's not the most discerning critter, growling at strangers and friends alike. So nix the guard-grudge and go for the heavy artillery: Adopt healthy boundaries that can protect you from at least a portion of the hurts destined to come your way.

Forgive Daily

If you're determined to unload a nuisance grudge, here's a tip: Forgive daily.

I don't know what we're thinking, but it's all too easy to get rid of a grudge, then six weeks or six months later find ourselves standing at the pet store or the pound, gazing wistfully at our former pet through the wire cage, considering unlocking the door and taking him home with us again.

I remember when I forgave my biggest hurt. Of course, it took half a decade of grudge ownership and two years of counseling before I could rid myself of my annoying pet. I had two really good years before my grudge found its way home, tail tucked, tongue lagging, eyes pleading. At first I just snuck some food out to him on the back porch. But within a couple months he was back in the house, comfortable again in his old spot under my bed.

I wish I could say getting rid of a grudge was a one-shot deal. But sometimes it's not. Sometimes it's a daily choice. It's saying, "I will forgive today," and saying it every day of your life if necessary.

Find a Mentor

Learning to let go of our grudges and forgive the friends, family, or strangers who have wounded us deeply is a tough assignment.

You know what can help?

Finding a mentor.

That's right. Hook up with someone who has walked a similar path, who knows what it's like to be wounded, and yet has discovered the secret to grudge-free living.

You might know someone like this. It might be someone at your office, in your church, or maybe a member of your own family. Questions you might ask this person include, "Were you ever bitter?" "How did you learn how to forgive?" "What's your relationship like now?" "How do you maintain your good attitude?" "How can you just 'let go' of the hurt, anger, and pain?" "Are you ever tempted to pick up the anger again?" "If so, what do you do about it?"

I've got an idea. As long as you're looking for a mentor, how about going right to the top? There's Someone who's a master at forgiveness. In fact, he's forgiven more mistakes, malevolence, and pure meanness than you can shake a stick at.

I'm talking, of course, about Jesus. At thirty-three years of age, he was brutally tortured to an untimely death. His dying words? "Father, forgive them, they don't know what they're doing."

This is the man who was asked, "How often should I forgive someone who offends me? Seven times?" and answered, "No! Not seven times. Seventy times seven!"

This is the man who taught his followers how to pray to God, saying, "Forgive us for our wrongdoing, even as we forgive those who have done wrong against us."

This is the man who died a bloody death and endured separation from God so that you and I could be forgiven for all the times we make rebellious choices in our lives.

See, if God is anything, he is fair. He put cosmic laws into place that demand justice for wrongdoing. And the punishment for rebellion is death. Spiritual death. Separation from God.

I am guilty. You are too.

But God loved us so very much, he let his own Son take our punishment, the punishment of being separated from God. How do we know that Jesus experienced separation from his Father? As he was dying, Jesus not only said, "Father, forgive them," but he also asked, "Father, why have you forsaken me?"

Jesus experienced separation from God. Jesus took on so many of our sins, the Bible says he *became* sin for our sake. His crimes — our crimes — were so many that his own Father could no longer stand the sight of him. He turned away. I imagine that he must have wept. The earth shook. The sun hid. Blackness consumed the earth.

Jesus was separated from God for a brief while so that you and I don't have to be

Meet the Master of Forgiveness

Never met Jesus? He's closer than you think. Make this your heartfelt prayer and see the difference he can make in your life:

Dear Jesus,

I feel so hurt when others wrong me, and yet I'm no angel either! Jesus, I am guilty of so many things. Most of all, I am guilty of spending years rejecting a relationship with you and with God. Until now, that is. Please forgive me for these sins. I accept the great sacrifice you made for me nearly 2,000 years ago. I understand that you served the sentence for my crimes, and all that remains is for me to accept what you did for me and ask you to be my Savior and Lord. I accept it now, Jesus. I want my life to be different from this day forward. I want to experience your presence in my life. And as hard as it is, I want to learn how to forgive others, just as you've forgiven me. Teach me, Jesus, how to live, in every sense of the word. In your name, Amen.

Now tell someone about your decision. Is there a friend or family member who has encouraged you in the past to pray this kind of prayer? Call him or her. For that matter, contact me! I would love to join you in celebrating your new relationship with the Master of Forgiveness. E-mail me at klinamen@flash.net or write me at P.O. Box 2673, Duncanville, TX 75138.

separated from God for eternity. After three days, Jesus opened his earthly eyes, shook off the grave clothes, and walked out of the tomb.

Sentence served. Case closed. You and I are free. Forgiven. Not guilty.

Does God hold a grudge? No way. The Bible says that once we turn over our sins to Jesus to be paid for with his death, God flings the memory of our sins into something he calls the "sea of forgetfulness."

Does Jesus hold a grudge? Nah. He says, "I've come so that you will have life, and abundant life at that!" Are these the words of a man holding a grudge? I don't think so!

Do you want to learn how to forgive? Seek out the Master, the Lord Jesus Christ. Your first lesson will be to experience the forgiveness that he offers. Give him your mistakes, your rebellious choices, your mean-spirited behavior. Feel the freedom that comes with the absolution that only Jesus can provide.

Then ask him to help you with your grudges. You know that abundant life Jesus promises? Well, abundant living is hard to come by when you're chained to a grudge.

Let go of the leash.

Learn to live.

Let Jesus show you how.

10

The Doctor Is In

Depression is serious business.

Which means it's okay to laugh about it.

It can be healing to see the humor in even the most dire circumstances. Laughter is therapeutic. It helps us cope and it helps us mend.

Unfortunately, I wasn't laughing when I was in the darkest season of my depression. I was pretty miserable.

How miserable was I?

One day Larry came home from work to find me melancholy on the couch, listening to a compact disc filled with music from the TV series *thirtysomething*.

"What's wrong?" he asked.

"I . . . I miss my friends!" I blurted.

"Our friends in California?" Larry said,

knowing that I hadn't really connected with anyone since our move to Texas.

"Well, yes, but actually I'm talking about Michael and Hope and Ellen and Nancy and . . ."

My husband stared as I rattled the names of the characters from a TV show that had been off the air for about six months. "Your . . . friends," he repeated slowly.

I nodded, tears springing to my eyes.

My depression was so isolating. I didn't have the interest or energy to pursue real relationships with real people. But somehow, in my bruised and empty world, I had forged a connection with a cast of friends who demanded little of me save my presence in front of the TV one hour each week.

The good news is that, at some level, I saw the absurdity of my problem. "Have you ever heard of such a crazy thing?" I wailed. "I mean, they're TV characters, for crying out loud. I can't believe I'm so upset! Am I insane or what!"

My husband, God bless him, didn't take the bait. Instead, he sat beside me and offered the only comforting words he could think of at the time.

"Karen, you're not crazy. Lots of people,

um . . . feel close to . . . you know . . . fictional characters or people they haven't, well, actually ever met. That doesn't mean they're crazy."

I started to feel better. "Really?"

"Sure."

I brightened some more. "Like who?"

He knitted his brows. "Let's see. Some examples might be . . . oh, I know! How about that guy who thought he spotted Elvis at a filling station in New Mexico? And I saw on TV last night a story about a couple who believe that alien beings have taken over the White House. So, see? You're not alone at all."

I sniffled and wiped my nose, eyeing my husband carefully over my tissue. "Let me get this straight," I finally said after a long pause. "You are putting me in the same category with people who think the First Lady is a Martian and Elvis is a gas jockey in the desert, and you think this is somehow supposed to make me feel better?"

Eventually Larry and I got a smile out of the incident.

Which is a good thing, since smiles were hard to come by in that season of our lives.

Trust me when I say that I was past the point where singing TV theme songs, calling a friend, or taking a minivacation were going to, in and of themselves, do me a whole lot of good.

It was time to break out the heavy artillery.

The Doctor Is In

"Minirth-Meier Clinic," a woman's upbeat voice said cheerily through the telephone receiver I clasped, white-knuckled, in my hand.

"Mynameiskarenlinamenandiwanttomakeanappointmentwithadoctor," I mumbled quickly into the phone.

"I'm sorry, could you repeat that?"

I sighed. This was going to be a lot harder than I thought. And yet, coexisting with my dread was a sense of relief. I was tired of carrying the burden by myself. I had stumbled around, blind and heavy laden, long enough. I hadn't found a door out of my prison. I couldn't even find a window or a mouse hole.

But here was something. It wasn't much, just a channel the width of a phone cable. I couldn't see any light at the end of it, but it had brought me a voice, the voice of someone who could hook me up with someone else who maybe, just maybe, knew of a secret path that I could take back into the light.

I took a deep breath. "My name is Karen Linamen, and I want to make an appointment to see a doctor."

They say a journey of a thousand miles begins with a single step.

Funny Farm or Healthy Choice?

Perhaps you, too, have found yourself in similar circumstances. It's also possible that you've experienced a slightly different version of "rock bottom," perhaps when a marriage died or a parent succumbed to a terminal illness or a child embraced a self-destructive lifestyle that left your heart (and your sanity) in shreds.

Chances are, most of us have experienced times in our lives when our burdens became too great to bear, and we longed for someone knowledgeable and kind to come alongside and help us carry the load until, together, we could find a suitable place to lay it down for good.

Friends and spouses and other members

of our family are often great sources of wisdom. But every now and then, what we really need is someone with not only wisdom, but a few years of formal training to boot.

It's hard to admit.

But there's no way around it.

Simply put, there are moments in life when you and I . . . well . . . we need professional help.

There. I said it.

Unfortunately, in some circles there's a stigma attached to the idea of professional help. It's as if, once we've admitted that we've sought the services of a shrink, acquaintances will visualize our closets lined with straightjackets or secretly wonder if those multivitamins we take daily are actually something stronger to help us remember that we aren't REALLY Joan of Arc or Cleopatra.

Give me a break. These are hardly the Dark Ages. Gone are the days when seeking professional help meant we had been spending too many hours in a dark room knitting with empty hands, or that we'd been spotted one too many mornings crowing naked from the roofs of our homes.

I know that for me, calling in the professionals was a turning point. The expertise that Dr. Robert Holmes brought to my situation was like beaming a flashlight into a very dark place, and illuminating a very thin trail back to wholeness.

Indeed, we don't hesitate to utilize the services of folks who have been trained to paint houses, dry-clean our clothes, or replace the struts on the family van. We hire accountants and piano teachers and even medical folks who went to school to learn how to diagnose ear infections and set a broken arm.

We pay for assistance from professors and plumbers, lawyers and landscapers.

Seems only natural to seek out the same level of expertise when we need a lasting repair for a wounded heart or broken spirit.

Let Your Fingers Do the Walking

So where do we find this kind of help?

Psychologists are one solution. Familiar with the anatomy of the heart and soul, these folks have heard it all and are prepared to help you in your quest for wholeness. Is it expensive? Sure. But hanging on to your pain is expensive too. Hanging on to your pain can cost you your health, your happiness, your marriage, career, or ministry — even the well-being of your children. If you seek counseling, you might want to check with your insurance company to help with the cost. I know our insurance company didn't cover things like marriage counseling. But because my depression was impacting my physical health in terms of appetite, sleep patterns, and stomach problems, our insurance company agreed to pay a significant percentage of the overall cost.

Psychiatrists are another part of the health-care community. While psychologists have gone to school to obtain their doctorate in psychology, psychiatrists have obtained their doctorate in medicine, which allows them to prescribe medication for depression and other maladies. If you seek out a psychologist, don't despair — if she perceives that medication is needed, she can refer you to a psychiatrist for one or two sessions to establish you on the dosage that will be right for you.

Marriage and family counselors have pursued specialization in issues relating to — duh — marriage and family. These folks come in varying educational packages: Some have doctoral degrees, some have master's degrees, and others are actually interns working toward their degrees. Their hourly rate will vary accordingly.

Here are some other options:

What about clergy? Many pastors allow time in their schedule to meet regularly with folks like you and me who are in need of some wise counsel.

If your problems are rooted in your marriage, there are wonderful weekend retreats dedicated to promoting healing and growth within marriage. An organization that you'll want to check out is Family-Life (http://www.familylife.com/index.html). Chances are, sometime in the next six months, a group such as this will be hosting a marriage conference within driving distance of your home.

When it comes to getting help from professional caregivers, you can find resources in the *Yellow Pages*, but an even better option is word of mouth. Talk to people you know who have experienced a measure of healing through the help of a professional. Ask them to describe their experience. What did they like about the choice they made? What didn't they like? Do they feel comfortable recommending their doctor or counselor or pastor to others?

Also, ask questions to see if the professional you are considering embraces values and convictions that are in line with your own. As a Christian, it was imperative to me that the man or woman I approached for help shared my faith in Jesus Christ and my belief in the inerrancy of God's Word.

A Footpath for One

I wish I could tell you, "Here are the nine steps I took to healing. Follow my path and you'll feel better too!" Unfortunately, I can't do that. And there are two reasons why.

First, I have no idea what path I took. All I know is that I stayed consistent about keeping my appointments with my counselor, even when I didn't want to go. On other days of the week, sometimes I cried out to God. Sometimes I just cried. I took three steps forward, then two steps back. One step forward, one step back. Four steps forward . . .

Then one day it dawned on me that, while I wasn't out of the woods quite yet, I was going to get there one day.

The Good News about Depression

Most people who suffer from clinical depression feel a sense of relief when they learn the facts about this medical illness. They realize that depression is not a personal weakness and that they are not alone — men and women from every walk of life, young and old, suffer from clinical depression. They are also relieved to know medical research has produced a variety of effective new medications to treat the illness. The National Institute of Mental Health estimates that 80 percent of people with clinical depression can now be successfully treated, usually with medication, psychotherapy, or a combination of both.

Use the following checklist to determine if you or someone you know is suffering from clinical depression. If five or more of the following symptoms have lasted for more than two weeks, tell a doctor as soon as possible. Only a qualified health professional can diagnose if someone has clinical depression. But knowing the symptoms of clinical depression can help you as you talk with your health professional.

Feelings of sadness and/or irritability

Loss of interest or pleasure in activities once enjoyed

Changes in weight or appetite

Changes in sleeping pattern

Feeling guilty, hopeless, or worthless

Inability to concentrate, remember things, or make decisions

Fatigue or loss of energy

Restlessness or decreased activity noticed by others

Thoughts of suicide or death

Used with permission from the National Mental Health Association (NMHA). For more information, call 800-228-1114 or visit their web site at http:// www.nmha.org/ccd/index.cfm.

So I can't really tell you the path I took. All I know is that it was a circuitous path that twisted and turned, wending beneath a dark canopy of gnarled limbs and sun-proof leaves. Sometimes my path was nearly invisible, buried beneath a soft carpet of moldy leaves. At other times I was startled by the sounds of living things scurrying along hidden paths in the undergrowth, and once I caught a glimpse of a dark shape darting ominously across the shadowy path that lay ahead.

I just kept walking. Did I have a choice? Turning back was even scarier than forging ahead. Day and night were the same, a perpetual twilight. The thick foliage was impartial, diffusing both sunlight and moonlight to the same sourceless shade of gray.

And then one day I saw a patch of dappled sunlight on a mossy stone. I could have stayed there forever, by that stone. Especially since the path ahead took a particularly dark turn. Reluctantly, I left the sunlight behind and pressed on toward the shadows, nursing a small hope that there would be more sunlight ahead.

Eventually there was. Entire meadows, in fact. Sunlight and gurgling brooks and flowers too.

I wish I could tell you how to take the path I took.

Unfortunately, Hansel and Gretel hold the copyright on that bread-crumb thing, and AAA has always fallen short when it comes to providing TripTiks for these kinds of locations.

Of course, the second reason I can't direct you down the path I took is that your path may be completely different than mine. In the journey toward inner wholeness, a vast wilderness beckons, and each pilgrim blazes a virgin trail.

But here's the good news. I got through the wilderness. I know you can too. I want to encourage you. There is life after depression. There is life after divorce, and after the death of a loved one, and after panic attacks and breakdowns and more.

If you are feeling overwhelmed with life, call a friend or plant a garden. If your feelings are starting to redefine who you are, or you can't break free no matter how hard you try, or you can't break free and you don't even care anymore, then call a professional. He or she can get you on the right path, and equip you with the resources you'll need along the way.

Needing help isn't a terrible thing. The real tragedy is not taking advantage of the resources that are available to lighten our load.

So the next time you find yourself crowing naked on the rooftop, talking to Elvis, or looking for E.T. during a State of the Nation address, don't hesitate a moment. Call someone well trained to handle cases just like yours.

And for the rest of us, here's a thought: While we're waiting for our next counseling appointment, we could always make friends with someone who thinks Bill Clinton is Jabba the Hut in disguise.

We'll feel *real* normal in comparison.

Tickle Your Inner Child

I just had a birthday. My friends went all out. Nancy cooked a succulent ham dinner, inviting five families to her home after church. She went so far as to decorate her house with festive spring colors. The dads even orchestrated a treasure hunt in the yard for the kids, hiding two hundred plastic eggs filled with candy. Kacie ate way too much sugar and caffeine. If I had just given her a dust rag, she could have cleaned ceiling fans while she was up there.

Imagine! All that festivity just for li'l ol' me. I'm sure the fact that my birthday happened to fall on Easter this year was hardly a factor at all.

So now I'm a year older.

I don't usually feel older after a birthday.

But this year I did. By the time I left the party I had this inexplicable craving for Metamucil. When I got home I kept punching the remote looking for Bowling for Dollars on cable. At bedtime my husband was in the mood for romance, but I wanted to save my strength — I've heard they have Monday morning bingo at the community center.

I haven't hit forty yet, but I'm in the neighborhood.

There's good news and bad news about birthdays. The good news is that we get presents . . . the bad news is that we get older. The good news is that people say nice things about us . . . the bad news is that our hearing isn't what it used to be and we can't be quite certain what they said. The good news is that we've reached a milestone . . . the bad news is that we're starting to show some mileage.

You know how they say you can't have your cake and eat it too? I'm discovering this is particularly applicable to birthday cakes. This is because, by the time we're thirty-five or so, our birthday cakes sustain so much fire damage it's questionable as to whether or not they're still edible.

Which is really a shame. I understand

that as you age, soft foods really come in handy.

You're Only as Old as You Feel

If you're only as old as you feel, there are days I must be approaching my centennial. I'm discovering that while beauty is only skin-deep, age can make you feel weary to the bone.

You know when I feel *really* old? When I'm feeling beat up by life in general. I don't need to be anywhere near my birthday — if I'm feeling stressed and overcommitted and overwhelmed, I'm feeling old.

I remember, when I was seeing a counselor for depression, explaining how dried up and lifeless I felt. I told him I was convinced my best years were long gone. I couldn't imagine feeling vivacious and energetic ever again.

He assured me this was my depression talking. He said people can "feel young" at any age. He even confessed that for his forty-eighth birthday he had requested, and received, a pair of roller blades.

I was tempted to ask if, for his forty-seventh birthday, he had requested, and received, a lobotomy.

I was also curious if he hoped to be out of traction by the time he turned forty-nine.

Actually, the man had a valid point. Outside stresses and inner turmoil can drain the life right out of you.

You want to know another instant ager? Overcommitment. When I burn the candle at both ends and end up feeling lethargic and tired, that makes me feel old too.

A couple weeks ago a friend talked me into starting a new exercise regimen with her. I think we were doomed from the start: I'm a night owl who stays up late, and she rises with the sparrows. For four days, I managed to drag myself out of bed at the appointed time, 5:30 A.M., and meet her on my front porch for an aerobic walk around the block.

One particular morning I realized I had made a huge mistake a couple hours after our walk. I had walked into the den to open the window shades. The next thing I knew, I woke to find myself draped over the back of our couch. I had been in the process of leaning over the couch to grab a shade when I dropped unceremoniously into a deep sleep.

I was either pushing myself too hard with this 5:30 stuff, or I had suddenly developed a very advanced case of narcolepsy.

Now I'll be the first to admit that exercise can make us feel younger. My problem was not the exercise, but the overcommitment. Those 5:30 mornings were simply not compatible with my 2:00 A.M. bedtimes. When we overbook our schedules in an unwise fashion, our energy and zest for living is often the thing to go.

So here's the equation: When we are "under the weather" physically, emotionally, or spiritually, we can find ourselves feeling like we've aged ten years overnight.

At the same time, when we feel tired and "old" of spirit, we're not really equipped to win the battle against the many forces that work against our physical, emotional, and spiritual well-being on a daily basis.

Unfortunately, the two dynamics work really well together, pulling and pushing each other into a perpetual pattern. The end result? We can easily find ourselves careening down the wrong road.

Want to break the momentum? Disrupt the pattern? Terminate the cycle?

It's as easy as child's play.

Get a Clue from a Kid

Ever notice how much energy children have? Granted, they're flinging around bodies that weigh twenty to sixty pounds while you and I weigh . . . Never mind, let's not go there.

But my point is that kids are indefatigable (I'd say look it up, except if you're like me you're too tired to hunt for the dictionary. It means *tireless*).

Wouldn't you love to bottle some of that energy? Just bottle it up, then take a swig whenever you were dragging. *Whizzang!* Suddenly you'd be Superwoman! If you were at work, your fingers would suddenly be flying on the keyboard at an amazing pace. At home? You'd have the beds made, dishes washed, socks darned, and chimney swept in the amount of time it used to take to fluff your pillow for your afternoon nap.

Coworkers would gape in amazement. Friends would gossip and stare. Your husband would request something for chest pains.

They'd be thrilled with your performance at work and the way your kitchen sparkled. But my guess is that sooner or later they'd question the Crayola scribbles in the hallway, the grass stains on the knees of your best pants suits, and the distracting way you'd have of jumping up and down, blowing spit bubbles, or picking your nose whenever someone was trying to get your attention.

So . . . maybe we don't *really* want all the energy of a kid.

Still, maybe we can pick up a few pointers from the little people in our lives.

Kids have such vitality. Such zest for life. They possess wild imaginations, boundless energy, and limitless passion. These are the things I miss from my youth. I don't know about you, but I would love to recapture some of the youthful zeal that characterized my life before grown-up responsibilities, problems, and anxieties got the better of me.

What secrets do kids have to share about youthful living (at any age)? What wisdom can we glean from their zestful ways?

Let's find out.

A Smile a Minute

A study recently revealed that children, on average, laugh four hundred times a day. On the other hand, in a given day adults laugh — are you sitting down? — about *fifteen* times.

Wow.

That means our kids are finding something to laugh about almost every other minute. You and I, on the other hand, are lucky if we chuckle once each waking hour.

You think we might be onto something here?

Do you want to feel younger?

Laugh.

I have a couple of assignments for you. Your first assignment is to make a list. Write down things that make you laugh. Is there a certain movie that tickles your fancy? Or a humorous writer? How about a favorite cartoonist?

Your second assignment is to, at some point today, find a way to incorporate extra laughter into your day. You can refer to your list, or improvise. Run out and rent or buy the video *Bill Cosby, Himself,* which features a classic comedy special Bill performed back in the early '80s. Tonight, turn on the Nickelodeon channel and watch *I Love Lucy* reruns on cable. Initiate a tickling match with your husband. Hand your kids loaded water guns (just keep the automatic twelve-gauge water rifle for yourself!).

Your third assignment is, well . . . a little zany. But I promise you won't regret trying it.

As kids, my sisters and I had this game. We would laugh. For no reason. One of us would begin the game by forcing a laugh. Not a "ha ha ha," mind you, but a "ha ha ha ha ha ha ha ha . . ."

The game has four stages. In the first stage (which usually lasts about five seconds) the person who starts the game is merely saying the word "ha" over and over. It sounds artificial. Fakey. Impotent.

The second stage commences as the laugher begins to feel the urge to apply some stomach muscles. She's not really laughing uncontrollably, but it's a pretty good imitation. It's coming from the gut. It sounds almost convincing.

The third stage (which is usually in full swing within a minute of the start of the game) is characterized by hysterical giggles, watery eyes, belly laughs, and even aching ribs. In this stage, the laugher has laughed herself into a state of genuine, uncontrolled, urgent, and howling hilarity.

During the fourth stage, everyone else in the room has succumbed to the contagion. Everyone is pink-cheeked from giggling, guffawing, and gasping for air between rounds of laughter.

Try this. If it doesn't work, write me at the P.O. box at the end of this book and I will prorate the cost of the book and, out of my very own pocket, refund every cent of the money you spent purchasing the two pages on which I've been recommending this activity.

One suggestion is that you try this when you're driving by yourself in the car. You won't look any sillier than the teenager in the next lane who is jiving and belting out the words to the tune on the radio, or the woman behind you who is talking on her cell phone, applying mascara, and changing lanes all at the same time.

Better yet, find a laughing partner. But don't try this with another grown-up. At least not until you've practiced a few times. Your best pointless-laughter-partner will be a kid. So seek out a son or daughter, or maybe a niece, or borrow a child from a neighbor if you must. Just find a willing cohort and "ha ha ha ha ha ha" until you see stars or need CPR, whichever comes first.

You won't have any idea why you're laughing.

But you'll be glad that you are.

Every day, children are engaged in the activity of expanding their horizons. It's part of their job description. Whether it's the hand-to-mouth action of a toddler, or the growing pains of our school-aged kids, or the experimentation of teen years, if there's one thing kids do and do well, it's yearn to get out there and experience all the world has to offer.

As parents, we encourage new experiences within safe boundaries. We pay for piano lessons and soccer uniforms. We send our kids to camp and to choir practice. We encourage them to try new and different foods (green beans qualify as a new and different food to some kids).

We open the door and nudge our kids into new territory even when our gut instinct is to hold them tightly at home. We might wring our hands when they attend their first slumber party . . . or wrestle with worry the first time they suit up for football practice . . . or watch the clock when they're out on a date . . . but we understand that exploring new worlds is a vital part of youthful years.

Sometimes the exploration brings pain and failure. Sometimes it brings amazement and joy. Sometimes it opens whole new vistas as our kids discover gifts and abilities, love and friendship, knowledge and opportunity they never even knew existed.

When we're young, every day holds the potential of countless surprises as we engage in the work of discovering unknown facets of our world, our relationships, and ourselves.

That's the great thing about being young.

It's also a key to staying young at heart.

Expand your horizons. Pursue new discoveries. Explore the world "out there," and your inner world as well, as you mine your soul for unknown wisdom, talents, interests, and abilities.

Take piano lessons for the very first time. Sign up for a watercolor class. Go back to school and finish your degree. Read a classic novel you never got around to reading as a kid. Visit an art museum. Learn to dance. Go to a restaurant and order something you've never eaten before. Entertain a foreign exchange student in your home. Volunteer at a soup kitchen, or undergo training to answer crisis hotline calls a couple hours each month.

If you aren't a churchgoer, seek out a

Christian fellowship near your home and see what they offer. Check out audiotapes from your local library and learn some phrases in a foreign language. Join a bowling league or a church baseball team. Organize a progressive dinner for neighbors on your block. Are you tempted to call a professional if a lightbulb needs changing? Then break out of the mold and tile the kitchen floor yourself.

You notice I didn't include bungee jumping. That's because even a rabble-rouser like myself has to have some standards.

But you get the idea.

Blast out of your comfort zone. Strive. Learn. Grow. Emerge. Expand. Explore.

It's a jungle out there.

Does that mean stay home? Not a chance. It just means pack a lunch.

Believe in Magic

Ever notice how kids see the world? Kids tend to be optimists and then some. They not only see the bright side; sometimes they see a little more than what's really there.

Kaitlyn's friend Rachel is a good

example of an optimist. One day she was telling Kaitlyn about a mutual friend who was learning to ice skate. When Rachel described how Jessica let go of the guardrail, lost her balance, and teetered precariously on her skates, Kaitlyn said breathlessly, "Did she catch herself?"

Rachel said thoughtfully, "Yes, she caught herself, but her rump was on the ground when she did."

Yes, kids are optimists.

They are also visionaries — sometimes they don't see what *is* as much as what *could be,* or maybe even what should have been. How else can you explain how a cardboard box can become a lifeboat, fort, and rocket ship all in the space of an hour? How else can you explain the belief that four packets of Kool-Aid, twenty Dixie cups, and a handmade sign can be levied into enough cash to buy a bicycle?

When they're little they believe in the tooth fairy and "cross my heart." When they're bigger they believe in Prince Charming and love at first sight. And there's even about ten years in there somewhere when they believe a hug and a Band-Aid can fix just about anything.

Kids believe there are monsters in the closets, and that four-leaf clovers are actually worth the search. And even when they get too old to admit it, they still believe if they get all the candles with one breath, their wish just might come true after all.

Kids believe in magic. What about you? What about me? If we want to feel ten years younger, we could take more vitamins. On the other hand, we could look for rainbows or wish on a star or put greater stock in the medicinal value of a hug.

Have grown-up problems and worries gotten the best of you? Tickle your inner child. Laugh. Grow. Believe. You'll be amazed how much better you'll feel.

Cross my heart.

It's All in Your Head

I've made a lot of confessions, haven't I? Between *Pillow Talk, Happily Ever After,* and even the book I wrote with Linda Holland — *Working Women, Workable Lives* — I've bared it all.

Okay, so maybe I've still got some secrets left.

But the point is, we've shared a lot, you and I.

And now I'm about to share something else. It's a story that proves two things. First, it proves that dementia is not always hereditary (crazy people don't necessarily get it from their parents, although many parents claim they get it from their kids). And second, it proves they don't make ovens like they used to. I'm talking about back in the days of The Brothers Grimm, when Black Forest artisans equipped household appliances with the kinds of little extras — such as added headroom — that made them so darned versatile.

It all started when Larry and I married and relocated from southern California to Anderson, Indiana. Our first home together was a house in a little subdivision surrounded by a sea of cornfields, six miles outside of town.

Now this might not seem like a big deal, but let me assure you that this was a major adjustment for me. Born and raised in a city that consumes half its state, the word "rural" wasn't even in my vocabulary. I had never even seen snow fall. I thought fireflies were legendary critters like Big Foot, only with better hygiene.

One day driving home from church I made Larry pull our car to the side of the road. This is because I'd seen, in a roadside field, a ewe nursing her lamb and I was excited to observe what was to me an unfamiliar ritual of animal husbandry. After all, in Los Angeles the closest thing we have to wool-producing mammals is the salesgirl in the sweater department at I. Magnins.

In any case, I was busy trying to adjust

to my new surroundings when this little problem began to emerge. It began when I found myself alone several nights each week while Larry attended class. There I was, in an unfamiliar house in a strange city and state — and out in the boondocks, no less! Before long my fears started getting the best of me. Isolated as we were, wouldn't our little house make an ideal target for robbers and rapists? What if someone tried to break in? Who could I call? Larry was in Muncie, forty minutes from home, and most every other soul I knew lived three thousand miles away, within spitting distance of The Magic Kingdom.

My imagination went into overdrive.

One night the doorbell rang. Fearing the worst, I looked frantically for something with which I could protect myself. Running to the kitchen, I grabbed the biggest butcher knife I could find. I was wielding it behind my back as I opened the front door a crack and peered out at my would-be assailants.

There on my front porch stood two Girl Scouts peddling Savanahs and Do-se-dos.

Another night I developed this inexplicable fear that someone was going to break in and . . . how shall I put this delicately?

. . . put me in the oven.

Now, I don't usually suffer from "home-a-phobia," but for some reason, during that season of my life, our little house seemed rife with danger. Although I didn't feel that any other major appliance in our home posed a serious threat, the oven gave me the heebie-jeebies. Maybe as a kid I'd read *Hansel and Gretel* one too many times. Maybe I was exhibiting the early signs of a deep-seated aversion to cooking that was destined to develop into a full-blown culinary dependence on Tuna Helper and canned peaches. Whatever the reason, my oven loomed sinister and threatening, an instrument of torture just waiting to be wielded by the next criminal mind that crossed the threshold of my home.

At one point, it dawned on me that my attacker might have a difficult time getting me to fit inside the oven. You will be relieved to know, however, that being the thorough researcher that I am, I opened the oven door and peered inside the cavity to evaluate the potential fit. It would be a tight squeeze, I decided. Unless, of course, I was no longer in one large piece.

So you can see that things — from a mental health standpoint — were getting entirely out of hand.

The whole thing came to a head one night when a bitter storm blew into town. Within minutes after Larry left for class, my situation had dissolved into a very nasty hostage situation of sorts, with me being held captive by my imagination which was, by that time, not only skittery with adrenaline but wearing an army jacket and ski mask.

I huddled in the kitchen as the winter storm raged outside. Buffeted on all sides by a howling wind, the little house whistled and rattled and creaked. I began to panic. What was that noise? Was it the wind — or something more sinister? If someone were drawing a glass cutter across a back bedroom window, would I recognize the sound? Or would I assume it was a wind-driven branch scratching at the glass?

I did the only thing an intelligent, fast-thinking, rational young woman could do: I got my butcher knife, backed myself into a corner, and stood frozen with fear for FORTY-FIVE MINUTES until I heard my husband's car in the garage.

Fear was ruining my life.

The Monster Thought That Ate Manhattan

Have you ever let a thought get the best of you?

It might be a scary thought, or an anxious thought, or even a jealous or lustful thought. But something happens, and before you know it, it's taken over your whole life.

I have a rosebush like that. It's on the west side of my house. It was there when we moved in. We've never watered, fertilized, or pruned it. In fact, since we're hardly ever on that side of the house, we've pretty much just ignored it.

I walked over there last week. The rosebush is the size of a Winnebago. Its top branches reach the bottom of a second story window. From side to side, it must be easily fifteen feet across. And it's deep too — maybe twelve, thirteen feet from front to back. It has tiny white roses. When it's in bloom, there are cascades of flowers, like a fountain. Or maybe like waterfalls tumbling down the side of a mountain.

This is the rosebush that ate Manhattan.

I have thoughts, however, that make my rosebush look like the work of a bonsai master. My thoughts might not have taken over the side of a house, but they've taken over my life. And unlike the rosebush, they don't have a wild beauty about them. Instead, these thoughts are all thorns. They cause discomfort and pain. Getting rid of them when they were little wouldn't have been much of a problem. But now they've grown far too large for me to really get a grip.

You know the kind of thoughts I'm talking about. My guess is that you've had them too. Thoughts that fall into this category include convictions like, "I can't do anything right." Or, "I'm such a failure." Or, "My marriage is doomed." Even, "I'll never get free of this depression."

Fears fall into this category too. Even an irrational fear can take over your life and rob you of joy and peace of mind. And what about those grass-is-always-greener thoughts about off-limit relationships? Those thoughts can be consuming as well.

Someone has said that you can't stop a bird from flying over your head, but you can keep it from making a nest in your hair. You and I have unwanted thoughts every day, don't we? Things that pop in our minds that could be obsessive or destructive if taken to an extreme. Do we let them wing on by? Or do we feed them and offer them a long-term lease?

When life seems crazy and out of control . . . when we're feeling stressed or blue . . . when we feel perpetually overwhelmed or mad or sad and we find ourselves wondering if this is as good as it gets . . . there are lots of things we can do to bring hope, sanity, and joy back into our lives.

One of our options is to examine our thoughts. Are we adding to our problems with our thoughts? Is it possible to improve our perspective and have our emotions respond in kind? Could a better attitude alter our circumstances? What resources can help us embrace healthier thinking? Let's find out.

Who Ya Gonna Call?

When you and I want to stop thinking unhealthy thoughts, one of our primary lines of defense is to — you won't believe how simple this is — stop thinking unhealthy thoughts.

You are no doubt thinking, "Ha! That's easy for you to say. You have obviously stopped thinking altogether, which means that unhealthy thoughts have been eradicated along with everything else, leaving you with the cognitive faculties of table salt."

But hear me out. Sometimes, if we can keep a thought out of our heads long enough, the power of that thought begins to wane. It just takes time. And discipline.

Eons ago I found myself in love with someone who was not meant for me. I needed to get over him. The good news is that I knew the passion would fade in time. The bad news is that, until it did, I found myself engaged in a civil war of sorts, with my worst enemy holed up in my own heart and mind. I thought of this man every day. In fact, many times each day. Let me assure you that this did nothing to hasten the healing process that would enable me to get on with my life and find lasting love and happiness with someone else.

I had to get him out of my head.

So I launched a campaign. Every time I had an unwanted thought, I pictured myself with a paintbrush in hand, painting a huge, sloppy red "X" across the image. It worked. Of course, I was busy banishing thoughts about this guy for months and months, but eventually the passage of time came to my aid and the power of that relationship began to fade.

I was intrigued to discover, while doing interviews for the book *Working Women, Workable Lives*, a woman who had used a very similar technique to rid herself of unhealthy thoughts regarding an adulterous relationship. She said this was one of the steps she took to withdraw from the emotional and physical attachment to a manager at the accounting firm where she worked. Here's what she had to say about the experience:

"I banned Randy from my thoughts. Every time I pictured his face, I imagined a big red circle with a slash — like the Ghostbusters' symbol or the 'No Smoking' sign — and mentally stamped it across my thoughts. I had to do it maybe twenty, thirty times a day at first. But it worked. Each time I used my 'Randy-buster' symbol, I managed to force him from my thoughts for that moment."

Change the Channel

There is another technique that can help us stop thinking unhealthy thoughts. It has to do with visualizing our minds as a television set, and then imagining that we are picking up the remote and switching the channel to more suitable programming.

Sure, this seems simple on the surface, but my guess is that married women will find this surprisingly difficult. This is because married women don't have any firsthand experience to draw on as they try to create this kind of scenario in their minds. Many married women have not, in fact, changed a television station in years. Indeed, many of them have never actually held the remote that came with their televisions when the sets were purchased back in the mid-'80s. The good news is that researchers are frantically working to develop techniques to surgically remove remote controls from the hands of husbands, but until the procedure is perfected, my advice to married women is this: Go to the home of an unmarried friend, pick up her remote, and practice changing the stations on her television set until you can get it right. Once you've mastered the technique, feel free to try the following suggestion the next time you need to make a "switch" to healthier thinking.

Jane Johnson Struck wrote about this technique in an excellent article that ran in *Today's Christian Woman* in January 1998.

In her article entitled "Time for a Change? How Subtracting from Your Life Can Actually Add to It," Jane wrote these words:

When my husband had to undergo biopsies for cancer, I was anxious. But once he completed radiation treatments and life went on, I really fell into the worry trap. I found myself worrying about our future, about doctors' visits, even about my own health and the health of our kids. Needless to say, my mind-set wreaked havoc on my mental and physical state — I became sluggish, depressed, filled with aches and pains. I knew I had to change.

So I hit on the idea of "fasting" from worry. I remembered some advice I'd given my daughter Sarah when she was in grade school. Every year when her school held "Fire Safety Week," Sarah would lie awake at night worrying about our house catching fire. "Mom, I can't sleep," she'd moan. "I'm worried about a fire. I can't get it out of my mind."

"Sarah," I'd tell her, "pretend your mind's a television set, and you're switching the channel. Now watch something happy, like family vacation memories!"

Years later, it was time to taste my own medicine. So each time I found worries swallowing up my thought life, I forced myself to change the channel. I'd intentionally focus on something concrete and pleasant — cardinals perched on the feeder, the winter sunset tinting the sky the frigid crimson — to blot out my preoccupation with "what ifs."

If worry's something you'd like to change about your life, try switching stations for a week. It will transform the way you feel.

Get to the Root of the Problem

In some cases, stamping out unwanted thoughts or learning to "change the channel" will work just fine. But sometimes, that's not going to be enough. This is because unhealthy thinking that occurs repeatedly along the same theme might signal a deeper problem or unmet need that should be examined.

If you're feeling exhausted from battling frequent negative thoughts related to, let's just say, your worth as a woman, then you might want to consider ways you can bolster your self-esteem.

If anger is your constant companion, you might begin by changing the channel, but if that doesn't work you might consider getting to the root of your anger — and learning some good anger management techniques — via counseling or some good books on the topic.

If your thinking feels clouded by depression, painting a Ghostbusters' slash and circle on your thoughts is probably going to fall short. What's at the root of your dilemma? Old hurts? A hormonal imbalance? If so, counseling and/or antidepressants may be your ticket back to wellness.

By identifying the root of destructive thoughts, we can often make the kinds of changes that will make healthy thinking possible at last.

Accentuate the Positive

Another tool that can help you and me win battles against unhealthy thinking has to do with giving ourselves better mental road maps.

The fact is, when we entertain images in our minds, we are tracing paths for our words, actions, choices — and even our bodies — to follow. This is why defeatist thinking is so dangerous.

For example, if we dwell repeatedly on our fears, our bodies will become accustomed to responding as though danger were imminent. As a result, we may very well fall victim to unpleasant physical side effects. Blood pressure, sleep patterns, eating behavior — even our immune systems — can all be impacted!

Or if we dwell, depressed and defeated, on our flaws, we may find ourselves repeating them unnecessarily. This is because we are wired to align our behavior with the mental pictures we hold of ourselves. If we picture ourselves as being "shy in group settings," we're less likely to override that image and speak up the next time we're in a group. If we define ourselves as "clumsy," our bodies will tend to follow suit. If we define ourselves as disorganized, then we will be more apt to tolerate disorganization in our lives.

But the good news is that this principle works in reverse as well. Picture yourself confident, and you'll feel more confident. Spend time imagining yourself organized and efficient, and it will be easier to put that kind of behavior into practice. Feeling stressed? Picture yourself calm and relaxed, maybe sitting on a beach somewhere, listening to the roar of the wind and waves as a loved one strums an old Eagles' ballad on his guitar. And guess what's going to happen to your body in real life? You're going to feel more relaxed.

My dad is a pilot who owns and flies his own plane. Many years ago he told me something that I've never forgotten. He said that, when you're bringing a plane in for a landing, it's real easy to get distracted by dangers on either side of the runway. There might be a river, or a ditch, or even a building — things you definitely want to steer clear of!

A lot of people think the best way to avoid these dangers is to keep them in sight. But the truth is, a pilot who keeps too close a watch on the path he's trying to avoid can find himself inadvertently drifting off course.

The best pilots scan the terrain and note where the dangers lie, but then keep their focus locked on the runway, letting their hands — and eventually the plane itself — follow the path that has been established by the eyes and mind.

There's a proverb that says, "As a man thinks in his heart, so is he."

Hide in your heart positive images about yourself, your marriage, your parenting, your strengths, and your talents. Regardless of the mistakes you've made in the past, if you keep your eyes on the course you want to take, you just might be surprised where you end up.

Think on These Things

Last but not least, fill your mind with God's Word.

Last weekend I spoke to the most wonderful group of women in Delhi, Louisiana. It was an amazing retreat. God orchestrated some real ministry, and I felt humbled and privileged to be able to come along for the ride.

But the entire week before the conference . . . well, that was another story as I was plagued with unusual stresses, temptations, and even fears. Was this spiritual warfare? Was Satan trying to get me distracted and off track for the weekend coming up?

I just knew that I had to clear my head of these unhealthy thoughts and regain my focus on what really mattered. I spent time that week in prayer. Then the Lord sent along several of my closest friends to pray for me as well. Finally, the morning of the retreat, Nancy — who had accompanied me — and I prayed together, and suddenly I was reminded of a verse in the Bible. It's found in Isaiah 26:3, to be exact: The Lord "will keep in perfect peace all those . . . whose thoughts turn often to the Lord!" (TLB).

That was it. The antidote to unhealthy thinking — fears, temptations, anxieties, and self-doubt — was to focus on Jesus. And one of the best ways I knew to do that was to focus on his Word as revealed in Scripture.

You know, there is power in the written and spoken Word of God. Jesus told his disciples that if they knew the truth, the truth would set them free.

And God's Word is nothing if it's not pure, unadulterated truth.

When we hide his Word in our hearts and minds, we are much less likely to be deceived into believing lies about ourselves, our marriages, our worth as human beings, even our purpose for living.

Oh yes. Back to our story. About my oven phobia . . .

Well, as I mentioned, I realized fear was ruining my life. Knives and mace might protect me from a flesh-and-blood intruder, but they were useless when it came to defending myself from my own fear. It was time to get tough and play rough. It was time to break out the heavy artillery.

The night after my oven delusion, Larry reluctantly readied himself for class. "Are you sure you'll be okay?" he asked a dozen times.

"I'm ready this time," I assured him as I waved him out the door. "I've got my secret weapon in place."

"Yeah, but last night —"

"Forget last night. I'm in control. I'm ready for the enemy."

No doubt Larry drove to school wondering how, in a small town in which I barely knew a soul, I'd managed to hook up with a black-market bazooka dealer.

In the kitchen, I began to clear the dinner dishes. Sliding them into the soapy water, I glanced up at the window over the sink. There, framed by the twilight, was an index card taped to the glass. I took a moment to read the words I had copied that afternoon: "For God did not give us a spirit of timidity, but a spirit of power, of love, and of self-discipline" (2 Tim. 1:7).

Later, pulling warm sheets from the

dryer, I stopped to read a card taped to the wall above the appliances: "Let the beloved of the Lord rest secure in him, for he shields him all day long" (Deut. 33:12).

And still later, as I went to the stereo to insert my favorite cassette, I read: "The Lord is faithful, and he will strengthen and protect you from the evil one" (2 Thess. 3:3).

When Larry pulled into the driveway that night around 11:00 P.M., I greeted him at the door with a smile instead of a knife.

The intruder had been conquered: not by mace, not by cutlery, but by the power of the Word of God.

Draw a Line in the Sand

Everybody's talking about boundaries. Mental health gurus, time management experts, parenting wizards, financial counselors, doctors, preachers, and teachers all extol the virtues of healthy boundaries. And I'm about to join their ranks.

This is because there's a lot of truth to the concept that there's nothing like healthy boundaries to keep life in check and stress at bay.

But before I dispense my advice, let me just say that advice-givers tend to fall into two categories: those who practice what they preach, and those who don't.

I, of course, am among the latter.

Confessions of the Boundary-Challenged

Boundaries? I know what boundaries are. Boundaries are those annoying things I'm in the habit of stepping over in the process of doing the things I want to do. Actually, that sounds more intentional than it really is. I'm not personally opposed to boundaries. I just get so enthused about whatever it is I'm doing, I tend to forget they exist.

I talk too much and laugh too loud and never go to bed at a reasonable hour. I spend too much on Christmas gifts and have been known to greet acquaintances with the kind of bear hugs usually reserved for family members who have just rejoined life on earth after spending seven years on a space lab based on Mars.

When I bake chocolate chip cookies, I figure if one cup of chips is a good thing, two cups must be even better. I've been known to bake cookies with such a high chocolate content that they're not only illegal in many states, but they have to be consumed with a spoon.

It's true that I can't say no to chocolate. I also have a hard time saying no to people. Room mothers, door-to-door steak salesmen, my children, Tupperware consultants, and Ed McMahon have figured this out and tend to use it to their advantage. I've paid for enough magazine subscriptions that I am expecting a personal thank-you note from the next person who wins the Publisher's Clearinghouse Sweepstakes.

Does this sound like I'm boundary-challenged to you?

Some friends and I held a garage sale last month. Three of us converged at Darla's house Friday morning bearing piles of discarded treasures. We spent most of the day sorting and pricing. We spent the next day haggling and selling. We worked hard. When I dragged myself home late that afternoon, Larry greeted me with a smile. "How much did you make?" he asked.

"Thirty-four dollars."

He blinked twice. "Thirty-four dollars?!? After all that work? Next time let me call Goodwill. We'll make more than that by making a donation and writing it off our taxes!"

I didn't have the heart to tell him that

while I was at the garage sale, I noticed that Nancy was selling a bag of Barbies and a box of really cool Christmas lights, and that Darla was peddling these great books and a jacket that looked just about Kaitlyn's size.

I didn't tell a lie. I really did make thirty-four dollars. Of course, I spent thirty-three shopping among the discards of my friends. At day's end, my net profits of two quarters and five dimes were jingling a mocking tune from my front pocket.

A person with better boundaries would have known better. A person with better boundaries would not have started her morning with the admirable intention of clearing out the garage, and ended the afternoon by backing a dump truck up to the house and hollering, "Let 'er go!"

I not only have no boundaries when it comes to finances and clutter, but I'm not particularly good with time restraints either. I am a devotee of the Linda Douglas school of thought when it comes to the overrated use of wristwatches. As my friend Linda has deftly observed, "But if I wear a watch, I won't have an excuse when I'm late."

This makes perfect sense to me. In fact, my eleven-year-old sets the alarm clock in the den to remind me when it's time for me to pick her up from school. This fact will no doubt provide fodder for a significant amount of discussion between Kaitlyn and her future therapist. But I try to look on the bright side. I have every confidence that Kaitlyn will be a good mother. I know this because she gets lots of practice mothering me. The other day she told me to put the caps back on the markers when I'm through using them. See? Another boundary I can't seem to grasp.

So why should you listen to a person with underdeveloped boundaries extol the virtues of boundaries?

For one thing, I'm a nonthreatening teacher. You will never have the opportunity to look at me and say, "But she's so 'together' she can't possibly know what it's like."

The other reason you should listen to me is because, as someone who struggles with setting healthy boundaries, I am personally acquainted with every conceivable pitfall, thus equipping me in an inexplicable and somewhat spurious manner to help you steer clear of danger and avoid a nasty fall of your own. Unfortunately, this is akin to asking a ski instructor with two broken legs to give you pointers on mastering

Deathwish Slope.

Still . . . if all the other ski instructors are busy at the moment . . .

Consider me the lone ski instructor on the mountain. So what if I'm not outstanding in the field? So what if I'm not usually even standing? The fact is, I've been down the slope a few times — even if it was on my rear — and you just might find my advice more valuable than you ever imagined.

Sorry. I'm rambling.

You know, better boundaries could have prevented that.

Boundaries Are Our Friends

There are some people who see a structured system of principles and boundaries and conclude: "Too confining. Not enough freedom." Some folks say this about religion. Some even say it about marriage.

And yet, the truth is that boundaries don't *eclipse* freedom; they *enable* freedom. Seriously, it's true. Boundaries are the very foundation upon which freedom and zestful, joyous living are built.

Seems paradoxical, doesn't it? And yet when we ignore healthy, commonsense boundaries today, we are very often narrowing our options for tomorrow.

For example, if I cross that chocolate boundary too many times today, I lose freedom in my closet tomorrow. I can no longer just walk in and pick something to wear, willy-nilly, from the rod. Oh no. Suddenly the field narrows, in contrast to my waist which is widening in such a manner that when I look in the mirror the words "continental drift" come abruptly to mind.

If I lose my temper with my husband and cross the boundary of healthy anger management (for some strange reason, the time I threw his alarm clock from our second story window comes to mind), I may very well lose freedom in my relationship with Larry. Indeed, my transgression could leave us both feeling resentful and hurt and withdrawn, a combination that tends to put joyous fellowship under lock and key.

If I can't adhere to reasonable boundaries when it comes to spending my money, I'm not going to have the financial options a few years from now that would have been secured by careful management today.

If I can't seem to say no to any request, project, or responsibility that comes my way, I'll soon find myself stressed and overcommitted. In fact, I'll be so busy trying to keep up, I'll no longer have the freedom to do a good job at anything, or to enjoy any of the projects or people in my life.

If I willingly let my thoughts and my emotions roam out-of-bounds — reading piles of romance novels, fantasizing about forbidden pleasures, or even flirting with relationships that are wrong or destructive — the near future may find me feeling trapped or even out of control. Indeed, my mind and emotions and even my actions can seem to take on a life of their own. Having made a choice to set these wheels in motion, the momentum may carry me well beyond any place I ever intended to go.

That's the bad news. The good news is that the principle works in reverse!

For example, healthy boundaries in marriage may afford me the freedom and privilege of celebrating a golden anniversary with a man with whom I'm still deeply in love.

Healthy boundaries when it comes to sleep, nutrition, and exercise will help me experience the physical freedom and energy that comes with a healthy body.

Emotional boundaries that protect me from toxic relationships may very well allow me to live free from the overinfluence of anger and depression.

Get the picture?

You know, for as long as I live I'll never forget how to spell *principal*, as in the principal of an elementary school, because my third grade teacher drove home the point that Mr. Larson, our school *principal*, was our *pal*.

I wish I could come up with something clever that could serve as a reminder that boundaries are our friends, but the word boundary simply cannot be rearranged into something meaningful like "pal" or "guardian angel" or even "Mr. Larson." Actually, the closest I seem to be able to come is the word *neibor*, as in "Like a good *neibor*, boundaries are there."

But maybe that's good enough.

Boundaries *are* good neighbors, after all.

Feeling Stressed? Check Your Perimeter

Often, when I'm feeling stressed or depressed, it dawns on me that I'm overdue for a boundary check.

Remember watching old westerns and seeing dusty cowboys on even dustier horses engage in something they called "riding the perimeter"? It was a process that could take days, depending on the size of the spread. Basically, these cowhands would ride around the edge of the ranch, making sure that the fencing was intact, and repairing any holes or breaks they found along the way.

See, these cowhands understood that in order to keep livestock safe and the wolves at bay, a sturdy boundary was necessary. And, unfortunately, boundaries aren't maintenance-free. They take some attention. Even some repair now and then.

Well, my world isn't all that unlike the sprawling spreads of yesteryear. In order to safeguard the good things in my life — and keep negative influences at bay — I need to make sure my boundaries are intact. And sometimes that means grabbing the toolbox for some necessary repairs.

Think about the healthy boundaries in your life. Are they in good working order? Perhaps a breach is allowing unhealthy influences into your world. If so, is there anything you can do to strengthen the fence and regain control in your life?

Are you allowing a relative to get away with frequent critical and cutting comments that leave you wounded?

Is someone at work making inappropriate comments to you, and you don't know how to get him to stop?

Do you have a friend who keeps you up to date on the latest gossip, despite the fact that afterwards you usually feel guilty about the things you said and heard?

Are you a "pleaser" who can't seem to say no to any request from friends, family, church, or work, no matter how inconvenient or obtrusive?

If so, you're not alone. And to encourage you (and maybe even provide you with some ideas on how to set better boundaries), I'd like to share some boundary ideas from women who drew lines in the sand and felt better about their lives as a result.

Boundary Checklist and Suggestions

Certain types of plants and flowers grow thick and lush in a pot or planter, but become straggly and pest-infested if allowed to roam free. Other plants — like the mint herb, for example — will run rampant and take over an entire garden without proper restraints. But when you give mint some boundaries (my friend Darla puts mint in a plastic pot, then buries the pot in her garden so the mint can thrive but roots can't spread out of control), it makes a welcome addition to any landscape.

In a similar manner, the following areas of our lives bloom best when nurtured with good boundaries:

Finances

Darla says she and Mike have a policy of sitting down together and discussing any potential purchase greater than fifty dollars. This not only keeps impulse spending at a minimum, but it also helps the couple stay reminded of their financial goals, and in tune with each other.

My husband is a savvy financial manager who refuses to carry a balance on a credit card. He never charges more than he can pay off when the bill arrives in the mail. In this way, he uses the credit card for cash

Is "Overcommitment" your middle name? Do you hate to turn anyone down? Do you say yes before thinking? If over-commitment is making you run behind schedule, here are ten ways to say, "Thanks, but no thanks":

1. "I'd love to, but this isn't a good time for me to make that kind of commitment."
2. "My plate's pretty full at the moment; I'm going to have to say no."
3. "Not this time."
4. "I'm going to have to pass."
5. "I can't be involved at this time. But let me make a recommendation of someone else who might be willing to help. Have you considered asking _____?"
6. "I wish I could say yes, but my schedule at the moment is filled to the brim."

7. "It would be a mistake for me to take on that project

right now because I don't have the time available to do the best job."

8. "Thanks, but no thanks."
9. "I cannot, in good conscience, make another commitment right now."
10. "No."

flow rather than for credit, enjoying convenience without the burden of exorbitant interest rates.

What financial boundaries do you currently observe?

Can you think of any additional boundaries that would benefit your bottom line?

Friendships

A friend of mine, I'll call her Terri, was pleased when her new neighbor seemed interested in striking up a friendship. Several times a week, in fact, Cindy called or dropped by to chat.

But several months later, the friendship was on the verge of becoming "too much." Cindy was coming by daily, and seemed offended when Terri had other commitments to family or friends. At one point, Terri remembers, Cindy even suggested the two families tear down the fence between their homes and create a shared "compound" of sorts.

Terri needed to set boundaries. But in addition, she needed to communicate to Cindy that she continued to value the friendship.

First, Terri looked at her schedule and decided how often she wanted to spend time with Cindy. She decided twice a week would be nice.

Then she took a twofold approach: First, she began saying no to excessive invitations from Cindy, making sure to agree to one or two engagements each week.

Second, she worked hard to beat Cindy to the punch whenever possible, taking the initiative to suggest shopping or lunch — while still keeping their get-togethers to a maximum of twice a week.

The combined strategy — setting limits and pursuing the friendship at the same time — brought the relationship into balance. The two women remain close friends today.

What's another healthy friendship boundary? How about this one: Darla has pointed out the importance of not tearing down your husband in front of your friends. Sure, women talk, and one of the things we talk about is frustrations in our marriages. But baring your soul to one or two friends is one thing — frequently belittling your husband in front of a group of friends is another. Sure, your husband isn't around to hear, but he's bound to notice that he's lost the respect of your friends, even if he doesn't know why.

What boundaries help keep your friendships healthy?

Are there other boundaries that you might want to adopt as well?

Verbal Boundaries

We can't stop people from saying hurtful things to us. Unfortunately, too often our response is one extreme or another: Either we blow up, rant, or say hurtful things back . . . or we suffer silently, accepting the arrows of their words without ever letting them know they've caused us pain.

A better approach is to begin by making sure you verbalize your boundary. You might say to a teenager, "Son, the way you spoke to me just now crossed the line. I know you're angry, but the words and tone that you just used appeared designed to wound me, rather than communicate your message."

Sometimes that's all that's needed. It might mean saying to a parent, "You really hurt my feelings when you made that comment about my parenting skills," or explaining to a husband, "Honey, I felt embarrassed when you brought up my credit card bill in front of all our friends," or even saying to a friend, "I know in the past we've always made jokes about my weight, but the truth is, those comments hurt and I'd feel a lot better if we'd avoid them in the future."

Sometimes that does the trick.

But if it doesn't and an abusive pattern remains intact, decide how you will protect yourself when your boundary is crossed again, and explain your new strategy to the friend or family member whose words can hurt.

How can you protect yourself? You might promise to say, "That comment crossed the line. You really hurt my feelings" — even if you are in front of friends. Or you might promise to leave the room and abandon the discussion until civil tones and words can be restored. Or you might decide that ending the friendship is the best way to protect yourself.

Rather than blow up or seethe, do you use healthy communication to let friends and family members know when their words or voice tones leave you feeling wounded?

How can you establish better boundaries in this area?

Housework

I read about one mom who told her family, "If you don't help clear the dinner dishes, then you will be responsible for fixing your own dinner the following night." She made it clear that kitchen duties were a team effort — if her family didn't carry their share of the workload, she would not feel obligated to carry hers.

My sister-in-law, Debbie, makes unloading the dishwasher her first project of the day. She says when the dishwasher is empty, it's easy to load dirty dishes throughout the day, keeping kitchen counters clean. On the other hand, a full dishwasher means stacks of dirty dishes in the sink by noon. It's amazing, she says, the difference it makes in the kitchen when she holds herself to that one, simple boundary.

What housekeeping rules or boundaries do you observe that are worth their weight in gold?

Are there areas of your home that feel out of control? What new boundaries might reign in the chaos and make your home a more comfortable place in which to live?

Love Your Body

A friend of mine was checking her e-mail when she accidentally opened an item of correspondence addressed to her nineteen-year-old son. She assured me that she closed the file as soon as she realized it wasn't addressed to her.

But in the fifteen minutes it took for this to occur, she couldn't help but read a rather disturbing phrase. The phrase was simply this: "I STILL CAN'T BELIEVE YOU GOT YOUR NIPPLE PIERCED!"

When my friend told me about this, we both responded like you would imagine two conservative, forty-year-old suburban moms would respond when faced with this kind of blatant, irresponsible behavior — behavior that characterizes so well the restless angst of Generation X.

We winced.

I crossed my arms over my chest.

"Ouch," we both said in unison.

"You know that had to hurt," she said.

I agreed. "I need an aspirin just thinking about it."

If I were to make a list of the top ten ways to abuse your body, nipple piercing would have to rule the list. Other candidates?

How about bungee jumping? Undergoing a root canal without any pain killer? Listening to rap music? Having your bikini line waxed?

What about eating too much at Thanksgiving? Staying up past 3 A.M. watching the Star Trek Marathon on the Sci-Fi Channel? Breaking for a ten-minute lunch on a stress-riddled day and scarfing down two chili dogs and a Diet Coke?

How about wearing high heels?

You might also be guilty of abusing your body if the extent of your exercise regimen consists of arm wrestling your husband for the TV remote . . . or if you burn the candle at both ends . . . or if you chain smoke or binge eat or consume enough caffeine to animate Al Gore.

Need a Little TLC?

I don't know about you, but when I'm in the throes of PMS, stress, or depression, my commitment to self-care goes out the window. When I'm in crisis, I tend to opt for the short-term warm-fuzzy rather than the long-term healthy choice. What will make me feel better NOW? A bag of M&M's? Oversleeping? Undersleeping? Vegging out for five hours in front of the TV? The latest fad diet consisting primarily of kiwi and pretzels? Resorting to cigarettes or alcohol or a misuse of prescription medication or even food?

Sometimes, when I get REALLY stressed, I fantasize about doing something that my husband thinks is the ultimate in body mistreatment. But I'm not so sure I agree. I think a tattoo would be kind of cool. Nothing big. Nothing visible to the masses, even. And nothing tacky — no anchors or snakes or names of former boyfriends. No, I would select something tasteful, like a flower or heart. And then I would put it someplace where the sun rarely shines.

A few years ago I vowed to fulfill this

fantasy by my fortieth birthday. Larry assures me that he will allow this to happen when Jerry Springer replaces Martha Stewart as the guru of gracious living.

We have two years remaining in which to settle this debate. I'll keep you posted.

You Are What You Eat

What would happen if, when we're feeling overwhelmed or blue, we made positive choices that actually nurtured our bodies? What if, instead of getting careless about taking care of ourselves, we elevated health and pampering to a new priority level?

How can we nurture our bodies? I've got three ideas. And we're going to start in the kitchen.

I saw a sign I liked recently. It said: "If we are what we eat, then I'm fast, cheap and easy." It's probably a good thing that we're not exactly what we eat. But the truth is that how we fuel our bodies does have a huge impact on the way we feel and think and function.

I know I've shared this before, but when I was in the process of working through my depression, I went for about six months without eating any added sugar or fat. I followed no other dietary rules. If I felt like eating three bananas and four pieces of toast (with fruit preserves, no butter) for breakfast, then that's what I ate. If I wanted the chef's salad and the prime rib for dinner, then guess what went down the hatch? But when it came to potato chips, cookies, sour cream, chocolate, whole milk, and other sugary or fatty culprits . . . I looked the other way. I lost seventeen pounds without even trying. But an even better result was that my thinking felt more focused than it had been in years, and my emotional repertoire grew by leaps and bounds as well. That numb, dull feeling I'd experienced for several years began to give way to brighter emotions, joy and anticipation among them.

You want to nurture your body and, for that matter, your emotions as well? Then make good nutrition a high priority in good times and in bad.

No Sweat

And what about exercise? Fact is, exercise is one of the best weapons against stress and even depression. Indeed, when I was originally diagnosed with clinical depression, the doctor handed me a prescription for Prozac and said, "Take this. But just as important, I want you to find a way to exercise three to five times a week for a minimum of forty minutes. As much good as the medication will do, the exercise will do that much and maybe more!"

Now, you have to understand that I once bought greeting cards for my friends that read, "I gave up jogging because it was bad for my health." The inside of the card explained: "My thighs rubbed together so much my underwear caught fire."

I'm the only person I know of who has failed high school P.E. We've all heard the pop philosophy "Why sweat the small stuff?" Well, my creed has always leaned toward, "Why sweat at all?"

So, you can see that I don't exactly qualify as a poster child for aerobic activity. Which is why what I'm about to say is so important.

Move. Breathe. Sweat. If I can learn to enjoy it, I know you can too. Best yet, the benefits cross all boundaries and will impact every area of your life! You'll not only experience greater beauty and strength, you'll find yourself thinking clearer and feeling happier as well. The fact is, exercise motivates your body to generate endorphins, which stimulate feelings of happiness and well-being. This is why my doctor prescribed a good workout along with my prescription medication: He knew that exercise had the power to alter my body chemistry and elevate my spirits.

Take an after-dinner stroll. Join a gym. Get a dog (preferably one with a small bladder who needs frequent walks around the block). Just find a way to get out of the house or away from your desk, and let a good workout nurture your body and your soul as well.

Reach Out and Touch Someone

What is it about a hug or a touch that works magic? A touch can soothe, arouse, or reassure. Touch can create an emotional bond. It can impart confidence and hope and worth. Love can be communicated through a touch, as can desire, comfort, and even acceptance.

Our skin craves contact.

The night Larry asked my folks for my

hand in marriage, the four of us ended the evening with a wonderful hour of conversation in my dad's office. During this time, my parents gave my husband a word of advice. Actually, it sounded a little more like instruction from a User's Manual. I guess they figured they'd better instruct him on the successful care and maintenance of a Scalf daughter (1960 model) since they would be signing my title over to him in a matter of months.

My mom said, "Larry, you have to know this about Karen. She needs a lot of affection. She seems to have this quota. I'd say, if you added it up, we're talking about a good hour of hugging and holding a day."

My dad agreed, "She's not kidding, son. About an hour."

My mom added, "She just doesn't do well without it."

I had to laugh. I hadn't really thought about it before, but my folks were right. I've always been a hugger, a shoulder-squeezer, a hand-holder. Touch says something, after all, that even words cannot.

When we're in crisis, how can we harness the healing power of touch? I've got a couple ideas.

The first is easy. Ask for hugs. Not from total strangers, mind you, but family members and same-gender friends are certainly fair game. Not sure how to do this? Try these six magic words: "I think I need a hug." Say them with a sigh. You'll get results, I promise. Another way to get a hug is to give one. Proper hugging etiquette demands that the huggee respond with some manner of like affection to the hugger. Voilà. You've just netted yourself a hug.

How else can we nurture our bodies, touch-wise? Why not a professional massage? Or why not invest in some nice bathtime brushes and sponges, scrubs and creams? Satisfy your body's natural craving for tactile stimulation every time you step into the shower.

And, of course, here is my personal favorite: The next time you're feeling stressed or depressed, nurture your body and your soul with an extravaganza of tactile celebration.

Make love!

Lovemaking is good for you. In fact, researchers continue to document a growing list of emotional, psychological, and physiological benefits that can be yours for the price of an enjoyable romp under the sheets. In my book *Pillow Talk*, I have this to say about all the different ways lovemaking can enhance your life:

Sexual intimacy, orgasm in particular, creates a tremendous surge of adrenaline. Hearts race, muscles contract, and when the show is over, the body melts in delicious and total relaxation. Stress is erased.

Intercourse . . . and in some cases, cuddling without intercourse . . . actually bolsters hormones that maximize general physical health. For example, studies show that women who make love at least once a week have higher levels of estrogen than women who don't. Among other things, estrogen lowers cholesterol, keeps the cardiovascular system running smoothly, makes our skin smoother, and helps prevent depression.

Frequent lovemaking also releases endorphins into our systems, which not only promotes an emotional sense of euphoria, but also results in increased T cells, white blood cells vital for healthy immune systems. Finally, sex makes us more alert, stimulating circulatory and nervous systems.

You know, even the old standby excuse of having a headache falls by the wayside when we take a close look at the benefits of lovemaking. In one study, a majority of women reported that lovemaking actually relieved the pain of migraine headaches.

Feeling stressed? Nurture your body. Eat right. Sweat well. Make love. And leave the nipple piercing for the youngsters.

15

Tend to Your Soul

We've had a lot of fun together, haven't we? We've sung all eight stanzas of the theme to *Gilligan's Island* . . . we've learned what eating an entire box of Cap'n Crunch cereal will do to the roof of your mouth . . . we've perfected the art of fine whining.

We've studied the care and feeding of our dreams and learned the pest control basics needed to successfully rid our homes of grudges.

We've even evaluated, through meticulous field research, the recommended protocol for when a woman backs over her husband's portable computer with her car. (Hint: Go to the mall for roughly two years or until your husband is struck on the head by falling space debris and gets amnesia, whichever comes first.)

Believe it or not, we've even learned what it means if you find yourself convinced, beyond a shadow of a doubt, that Bill Clinton is actually an alien being from outer space (Kenneth Starr will be pestering me for your phone number, is what it actually means).

Of course, what I'm hoping is this: I'm hoping that through it all, you've gained some insights into strategies that can help you recapture a measure of sanity and joy the next time you're feeling stressed or depressed or facing PMS.

But here's the thing.

As good as these ideas happen to be, there are times that all this is far from enough, right? We can have a great network of friends, we can sing TV theme songs until we need CPR, we can take minivacations and prune overgrown thoughts and enforce healthy boundaries, but there will still be moments in our lives when we need something more.

Sometimes when we're feeling overwhelmed by life, we need to break out the heavy artillery, don't we? We need a no-fail-big-guns-sure-fire-money-back-idiot-proof-Arnold-Schwarzenegger-Wonder-Bra kind of a plan. In other words, we need a consistently powerful strategy that won't let us down no matter what.

What can bring us comfort when even chocolate can't?

How about the careful tending of our souls?

Give Me That Ol' Time Religion

Throughout the ages, religion has brought people comfort in even the most dire circumstances. And is it any wonder? We are spiritual beings, after all, and there is a facet of ourselves that can only be nurtured through channels that recognize this dimension.

Our souls are designed to worship something. Anything. If it's not God, it might be our kids or nature or material goods or patron saints or chocolate or our jobs or — we'd do well to move to India for this one — even cows. If you're not sure what you worship, Gwen Shamblin has a good definition. She says, "Whatever you go to when you need comfort . . . that's your god."

I don't know what you worship. Whatever it is, I hope it brings you the maximum comfort possible.

But in case it ever fails you, in case your soul starts feeling empty and deprived no matter how often you're in church . . . or on the Sunday school committee . . . or communing with nature . . . or chanting mantras . . . or lighting candles . . . or even handing your husband's MasterCard to ecstatic, chuckling salespersons at the mall . . .

Then maybe you'll want to try what works for me.

Fall in Love with Love

I mentioned earlier that the soul was designed to worship. I might even go so far as to define worship, in some fashion, as "falling in love." In fact, it's not unusual to hear someone say of young lovers, "He worships the ground she walks on," or of unspoken love, "She worships him from afar."

Think back with me a moment. Falling in love. Wasn't that an awesome feeling? It changes everything, doesn't it? When you're falling in love, nothing else matters. The earth moves. Birds sing. Stars spin.

Angels dance and fireworks soar.

Not to mention that thing that happens to your taste buds. I think Jenny Craig would do well to drop the nutrition angle and open an escort service instead. Nothing kinky. Just pair up a weight-conscious woman with a handsome escort for a couple months and see what happens. Move over Ding Dongs. Hello tofu.

My point is that nothing realigns your world like falling in love.

Now, given the fact that our souls were designed to be in love, we can try to meet that need by developing an affinity for all sorts of things that are sort of spiritual in nature: We can devote ourselves to theology, religious traditions, good works, even religious icons past and present. We can tend to our souls via devotion to humanitarian concerns. We can commune with trees and consult the stars. We can worship our inner children, wear crystals, and even swear allegiance to a denomination.

But we can't *fall in love* with these things. To fall in love, we need a person.

You want to rock your world?

Fall in love with Jesus.

It's about Time

On the surface, this may very well seem easier said than done. How do we, after all, fall in love with someone we can't even *see?* Sure, Demi Moore was in love with someone invisible in the movie *Ghost,* but we're talking Patrick Swayze here. Demi knew what he *really* looked like — even when he bore a somewhat disturbing resemblance to Whoopi Goldberg — and besides, if she experienced a temporary memory lapse she could always cough up three bucks and rent *Roadhouse.*

You and I, of course, don't have that kind of advantage.

So how do we fall in love with Jesus?

Well, how do we fall in love with anyone? Even if a potential lover can be perceived by our five senses, what is the pathway by which he is allowed to access the most intimate places in our very souls?

It's called time.

Of course, we don't fall in love with every person with whom we spend an inordinate amount of time.

But there's no doubt that every person we have loved represents a big chunk of our time. When we're falling in love, we're either spending time together, thinking about the times we've been together, planning the next time we can be together, or pining over the fact that we can't be together as often as we'd like.

Falling in love means spending time.

How can we spend more time with Jesus? Let's find out.

Read His Letters

Often people who know me personally will tell me that reading one of my books is just like having a conversation with me. They say they can practically hear my voice as they read my words, because so much of who I am comes through. Other people meeting me for the first time tell me they felt they knew me after reading one of my books.

You want to spend time with Jesus? Read the Bible. You'll not only learn about Jesus, but you'll read his own words, see his actions, hear his intimate thoughts, get to know his personality, and see his truths at work. In fact, the entire New Testament is composed of letters. On the surface, these may seem like letters written by itinerant preachers to people and churches they left behind, but if you want to know the truth — the honest to You-Know-Who truth — these are letters written by God's own Holy Spirit to . . . (drum roll here) . . . you.

So read his letters. You'll be spending time with Jesus as you do.

Praise and Worship

The Bible tells us an amazing secret.

It says that "the Lord inhabits the praises of his people."

Inhabits. Dwells. Resides in.

If you are singing praise songs to Jesus, or just closing your eyes and thanking him for all the ways he has changed your life, or sitting quietly and meditating as you listen to a tape of praise and worship songs . . . guess what? Jesus is there. With you. In the room.

Worship Jesus. It's time well spent.

Keep a Spiritual Journal

How else can we spend time with Jesus? How about by keeping a spiritual journal?

Imagine each time you sit down to write that you are sitting down with Jesus . . . because you are.

Now, I'll be the first to admit that sitting down in front of a blank page can be really intimidating. I'm a writer, for crying out loud, and even *I* can be intimidated by a blank page — I'm surprised the rest of you don't need therapy.

But I have a solution.

What if we made a schedule? What if we planned out, ahead of time, a "theme" for each day of the week? Then we wouldn't have to stare at an empty sheet of paper and wonder what we were going to write about that day. We'd have something in place to get us jump-started.

What if we followed a schedule something like this:

Sunday — Sermon notes. Take your journal to church and jot notes from all that wonderful teaching coming from the pulpit.

Monday — Write a letter to Jesus. Could be about anything. Begin "Dear Jesus," and end "Love, Me," and fill up the middle with whatever's on your mind. Tell him about your daughter's report card, your bowling league triumph, the fight you had with your best friend. Tell him about your sister's pregnancy. About the auto shop bill for the van. About what you're planning on making for dinner that night. Just chat. If the letter turns serious, fine. If not, that's fine, too. It'll be like real life, just a visit with a friend.

Tuesday — Rewind your mental video camera. Check out your memory archives. Think into your past and recall a moment when God seemed particularly close. Maybe even a spiritual milestone. Write about it. Here are some examples:

Did you used to dream about Jesus when you were a child? Did you have a Sunday school teacher who made a big impact on your life? Did you pray once for a puppy — and get one the next week? When were you confirmed or baptized? Did you accept Jesus at a summer camp?

Remember the first time you fasted and prayed? Did it change you in some way or give you new insights into the Christian walk? Did an accident nearly claim your life . . . and you walked away knowing that an angel or God or Someone up there was watching out for you? Did someone ever tell you about Jesus and — even though you weren't ready to receive him in your life — in your heart of hearts you knew that what you heard was true?

Were you ever experiencing a time of loneliness and turmoil — then suddenly saw something that made you realize Someone cared for you? I was feeling exactly this way one day when I looked up and saw an *intact double rainbow* stretched across the sky. Two rainbows, one on top of the other, each with both ends planted on *terra firma*. That would be four pots of gold, my friend. What an amazing sight. And I remember looking into the sky and knowing that I was loved.

Spiritual mysteries, moments, and milestones. Write about them.

Wednesday — What are you thankful for? Count your blessings. Make a list.

Thursday — Think about your world. Is it snowing outside? Does the amazing makeup of the snowflakes say anything to you about who God is? Is a robin building a spring nest? Does this bring to mind the verse in Matthew that points out that God cares about each little bird, and that he cares for you even more? Did it break your heart to say no to a teen's heartfelt plea today? Can that experience teach you anything about how God sometimes says no to you and me just because he loves us and wants to protect us from harm? Write about your world, and what your world can teach you about God if you just take the time to listen and learn.

Friday — Keep a running list of things you've prayed for, and how God is answering those prayers.

Saturday — Talk about your week. What struggles, heartbreaks, insights, small blessings, or miracles have been a part of your life this week?

Spend Time with Mutual Friends

If you want to fall more deeply in love with Jesus, then spend time with mutual friends. You can hear all sorts of encouraging comments and stories about your Beloved when you hang with others who know him well.

What does this look like in everyday experience?

Get involved with a close-knit group made up of people who share a relationship with Jesus. It might be a Sunday school group, or a Bible study, or an informal group of friends. My Friday Morning Breakfast Club has become that kind of group. I share a lot more than Cracker Barrel sausage patties, gardening tips, and Dave Barry clippings with the four women I meet with weekly. We share Jesus, too, and I know we've all grown closer to him as a result.

Something else happens when we spend

time with other Christians, especially when we drop our guard and communicate our vulnerabilities.

What happens is this:

The invisible Lover of our souls — the Jesus we love, but cannot see — suddenly finds himself in possession of a body. He has arms to hold us. Eyes with which to gaze lovingly into our own. A voice with which to call our names.

He has fingers to dial our phone numbers and vocal chords that can say, "I missed you in church last week. Are you doing okay?"

When we're feeling sick, Jesus has hands that smell like onions from preparing meat loaf, and sturdy legs that help him carry that meat loaf from the trunk of his car, up the driveway, and into our kitchens.

And when our hearts are breaking, he's got a shoulder we can cry on. And arms to hold us tight. And even his own tears to shed.

And Jesus isn't so invisible anymore, is he?

You know, throughout the New Testament, the church is given a crazy name.

It's called the body of Christ.

But to experience Jesus in this tangible, sensory way, our best bet is to place ourselves within the context of a loving Christian fellowship. (Which, if you think about it, is a far sight better than Whoopi Goldberg!)

Learn to Hear His Voice

Okay, one last thought on falling in love with Jesus.

And it has to do with learning to hear his voice.

You know, we live in a noisy world, don't we? We get in the car and turn on the radio. We walk in our homes and flip on the TV. We step into an elevator and the guy next to us is negotiating the price of widgets on his cell phone. Our lives are filled with voices and sounds, and that doesn't even take into consideration all the *visual* noise that comes our way. Seems something is always hollering for our attention: billboards, commercials, music videos, computer screens, etc.

If we were counting junk mail, my mailbox would be a sixty-piece marching band.

Noise.

Yet the Bible says, "Be still, and know that I am God." Are we quiet and still enough to learn the sound of his voice?

When we pray, is it a one-sided conversation? Are we doing all the talking? Or are there moments of silence, moments when we are simply quiet before the Lord, listening and experiencing his presence with us and within us?

What does Jesus' voice sound like? Well, if we've been reading our Bibles, we'll know. Jesus' voice sounds the same in our hearts as it does in the pages of his Word. If, during your quiet time, you think you hear him saying something that does not line up with what he's been telling you in Scripture, then that's not Jesus. If, for example, you feel you're getting a message from the Lord that you are worthless and he doesn't want anything to do with you, then guess what? That's not his voice.

Reading God's Word is like fine-tuning your antennae to the wavelength of his voice.

So be still. Read his Word. Listen with your heart. Learn to recognize and be comforted by his voice.

You know, Kacie is three now. But when she was a baby, she used to wake up from her nap crying for help. She'd be wet and hungry and alone in a dark room. Not pleasant stuff, I can assure you. And she would let me know, in no uncertain terms, that she needed me.

And always, hearing her cries from downstairs, I would drop whatever I was doing and head her way. And as I did, I'd be calling her name. "Kacie," I'd call. "I'm coming. Mama's coming. Everything's okay, Kacie. I'm on my way."

Calling loudly as you are walking up stairs is good for the lungs. Which is nice, because it means I got some small benefit from the exercise. All I know is that *Kacie* never seemed to benefit. No matter what I called out to her, Kacie would continue crying until I arrived at her crib and scooped her in my arms.

Undaunted, I continued this ritual every day. Even in the middle of the night when she awoke, I would make my way to her bed, yawning, talking, comforting with my voice long before I was there to meet her needs. And always she kept crying.

I remember the day it all changed. She was maybe several months old and, as usual, I was heading up the stairs calling her name when something happened that had never happened before.

She stopped crying.

She had heard my voice, listened to my voice, and trusted that I was aware of her discomfort and was in the process of answering her cries. Then she waited quietly, resting in that trust, until I appeared and drew her into my arms.

I don't know about you, but I want to be like Kacie. In the Book of Matthew, we are told to come to Jesus as little children. I want to do that. I want to learn to recognize the voice of my Father, and to wait patiently even when I'm uncomfortable, resting in the knowledge that he is preparing to meet my needs.

What about you?

Is he calling your name?

Maybe your circumstances still look the same. Maybe, like Kacie, you are in the middle of a crisis, your diaper wet, your tummy growling, your surroundings dark and lonely.

Yet when you learn to recognize his voice, you will find comfort. Jesus is trustworthy. He loves you. He knows what's best for you. And he will not forsake or abandon you.

Ever.